STENDHAL

ALSO BY WALLACE FOWLIE

*Climate of Violence: the French Literary Tradition from
Baudelaire to the Present*
André Gide: His Life and Art • *The French Critic, 1549–1967*
Age of Surrealism • *Jean Cocteau: the History of a Poet's Age*
Love in Literature • *Paul Claudel* • *A Reading of Proust*
Mallarmé • *Rimbaud: a Critical Study*
A Guide to Contemporary French Literature
Dionysus in Paris: a Guide to Contemporary French Theatre

MASTERS OF WORLD LITERATURE SERIES

LOUIS KRONENBERGER, GENERAL EDITOR

STENDHAL

❖❀❖❀❖❀❖❀❖❀❖❀❖❀❖❀❖

by Wallace Fowlie

THE MACMILLAN COMPANY

COLLIER-MACMILLAN LIMITED, LONDON

FIRST PRINTING

The Macmillan Company
Collier-Macmillan Canada Ltd., Toronto, Ontario
Printed in the United States of America

Contents

Foreword

At least three of the greatest writers France has known came in the wake of the Revolution and the Empire and wrote their first works at the time of the Bourbon Restoration of a monarchy largely dominated by the new bourgeoisie: Stendhal, Balzac and Baudelaire. Stendhal died in 1842. One hundred years later, at the time of the German Occupation, only one new novel, *L'Etranger* by Camus, reached a very wide audience. During those difficult years, and since that time, during the Fourth and Fifth Republics, French readers have tended to read and reread Stendhal, Balzac and Proust, rather than those novelists who were extensively read during the period between the two wars: Mauriac, Malraux, Bernanos, Céline, Giono, Montherlant.

This present study is an attempt to explain the resurgence of interest in Stendhal and the continuing effect he has on readers of his novels in France and outside of France. Critics constantly today speak of Stendhal, Balzac and Proust as the leading French novelists. Of the three, Stendhal often seems the youngest today, the novelist who speaks directly to the new generation of readers, especially in France, England and America.

Periodically the novel as a literary form is attacked as being too amorphous, too nondescript, too contrived by its omniscient author. Stendhal can be held up as an example to offset such criticism. He was the novelist living in a given society at a given period in history who was able to capture the feelings of his age, its problems and its weaknesses, and translate them into a language that was vibrant enough to last through four generations following his death. His personality is everywhere reflected on his pages, and that is probably why his personality has been more studied than his novels. This trend in criticism has changed today, and now the novels are being closely scrutinized in themselves, as exceptional works of art.

However, the novel is, for Stendhal, fictional autobiography. The life of the man and the art of the novelist are as difficult to dissociate as they are in the case of Proust. Fiction was self-expression for Stendhal and Proust more than for most novelists. Stendhal's pleasure in travesty was as strong as Proust's in pastiche. Neither Stendhal nor Proust tried to express in his writings a vain originality. Their subject matter, although personal in many ways, is common to all readers, and understandable in its universality.

Novels have been written in France for five centuries. How does one explain the survival of those few novels that continue to be read and that continue to count in the lives of new readers? Gide gave perhaps the best answer to this question when he said that the test of a good novel is its power to change the reader's feelings and condition. In recent years, Michel Butor, an admirer of Joyce, claimed that his biography would not be the same before reading *Finnegans Wake* as after reading the work.

During the past quarter of a century the novel has continued to be a prosperous literary genre, although in France it has been surpassed in poetry, plays and criticism. No other genre possesses the rich potentialities of the novel. It is founded on knowledge, experience and meditation. Characters in the novels of Sartre, Genet and Beckett speak more profoundly about their world, today's world, than historical documents and surveys and interviews. In the novels of Stendhal the written word is a gauge on the world of his day, and it is at the same time a creation that goes beyond a mere testimonial of his day. As we read *Le Rouge et le Noir,* we learn a great deal about the Restoration, but we also begin to feel that we are no longer outcasts in our own lives. The novel, in its highest instances, in *La Chartreuse de Parme,* in *Le Temps Retrouvé* is that form where human day, and it is at the same time a creation that goes beyond life takes on its clearest meaning from a fable, from a story. It is that literary form, more than a poem or a play, that is concerned with the complexities of human life, with the multiple daily realities that add a further dimension to the inexhaustible myth of human life. The novel will doubtless continue to last as long as man feels the need to explain his presence in the world.

Anyone who writes on Stendhal today owes so much to historians, scholars and critics, that it is impossible to list all acknowledgments. Stendhal has become an institution in our time, with the Stendhal Club in Grenoble, presided over by Vittorio del Litto, with the editing of Henri Martineau, with the exemplary contributions of Léon Blum, Paul Arbalet, Jean Prévost, Maurice Bardèche. At various points in my study, I indicate specific critical illuminations that have helped me, but it is impossible to acknowledge everything. The bibliography is a listing of those works that have contributed the most to my own understanding of Stendhal.

I began the actual writing of this book in the summer of 1967, when I worked at Yaddo, in Saratoga Springs, and I wish to express here my appreciation to the Yaddo Corporation for its hospitality. Thanks to a grant from the Duke University Research Council, I did some of the final work on the first draft, in the summer of 1968, in places associated with Stendhal: in Naples, first, and then in Grenoble. Finally, I would like to thank Louis Kronenberger for his invitation to write this book for the Masters of World Literature Series.

W.F.

STENDHAL

Henri Beyle

IT WOULD BE FOOLHARDY to attempt to reduce Stendhal's character to anything that is simple or straightforward or clear. He was the opposite of all that, in his role of rebel, in his everlasting need to distinguish himself from others, to have himself characterized by singular attainments. He refused to be one person, because for himself he was not a man related to one place and one family and one career. He moved about more than most writers, changing addresses with the frequency of an actor on tour. And he changed loyalties with the versatility of a man who fears attachments or feels he has no talent for attachments. This changeableness of place and sentiments induced such changeableness of nature that he was forced to accept the fact of contradiction in his life and thought. But contradictions led to more varied experiences, and these he welcomed.

Stendhal's life and character never come to an end for his biographers and critics. They never came to an end for himself as a writer, because they are the sources of all his books, and he hardly tapped their deep resources. What he told about himself was one thing, and what he concealed about himself was something else, something that can only be guessed at now. He was skillful in covering up his tracks, in changing his name and address, in throwing the hunters off the scent, in escaping to other cities where his life of love and ambition and society might resume or start over again. The details of such a life are as numerous as are the changes of temperament. They are useful to know only in as far as they help to demonstrate the principal lineaments of a literary work, as well as those traits of character that return the most often during life and therefore seem to be the closest to the truth.

Everything is strange about Stendhal. It is not usual, for example, to have to search for a man's authenticity in the many disguises he deliberately adopted, and it is not usual for a literary work to be practically meaningless for the writer's age and then eighty to a hundred years later to coincide almost exactly with the attitudes and the thinking of another age. For the past fifty years, in France and elsewhere, but especially in Italy, England and America, Stendhal has been looked upon as a writer who speaks directly to his audience, who seems contemporary in his way of thinking, in his estimates of human life and society and those drives that shape a personality. Those who continue rereading Stendhal form a kind of society. For countless judicious readers of literature, he is the writer par excellence, and, even more than that, he is a spiritual brother.

This youthfulness of his work is its miracle and its mystery. He wrote *Armance* at the age of forty-four, *Le Rouge et le Noir* at forty-seven, *La Chartreuse de Parme* at fifty-six. These are three books about young men, about their first impressions of life, about the first ideas that stir their faculties, about their first awareness of the stirring of their senses and their sensuality. Stendhal's young readers are able to identify with Octave, Julien and Fabrice, and older readers are spellbound by the intelligence and the accuracy of these recordings. Throughout his life, Stendhal saw with the eyes of a young man. His books are the stories of the aspirations and disappointments of young men.

Henri Beyle (Stendhal was a pseudonym) reached Paris a few days before the end of the century, in November 1799. He was almost seventeen, since he was born on January 23, 1783. He had spent his first sixteen years in a fairly well-to-do bourgeois family in Grenoble, a city of 25,000 inhabitants. His father, Chérubin Beyle, was a barrister in the Grenoble parliament, a man destined to become one day the deputy mayor of the city. Stendhal gives a more than unfortunate portrait of his father in his *Vie de Henry Brulard*.

Chérubin's wife, Henriette Gagnon, was the daughter of the physician Henri Gagnon. Stendhal liked to imagine that his mother's family was of Italian descent. If the father's reputation suffered from the caustic criticism of the son, the mother, who died when Henri was seven, was transfigured in the autobiographical work into an admirable figure of beauty and sensitivity and intelligence. To speak of an Oedipal complex is understandable, and countless critics have done so. There is no doubt the boy worshipped his mother and sustained for years what resembled a veritable cult for her. Her father, Dr. Gagnon, was a cultivated man and was responsible for his daughter growing up with some feelings for the arts. In his estimate of his two family traditions, Stendhal will be harsh on the Beyles, who came from the plateaux of Vercors in the Dauphiné, and admiring of the Gagnons, whom he claimed descended from a Guadagni family that had followed the papacy from Italy to Avignon. Such a hypothesis delighted him. He liked to think of himself as resembling his mother and continuing her Italian traits and temperament.

After his mother's death in 1790, everything grew hostile to him at home: his father's ideas and manners and love for money. He refused his father's affection and turned to his grandfather Gagnon whom he called his *véritable père,* and in whose house he spent as much time as possible. At the corner of the Place Grenette and La Grande Rue this large house had a terrace that was part of ramparts built by the Romans, where the family used to congregate on summer evenings. Alone with his grandfather, the boy often watched the sun set and the coming of night over the mountains. Only one member of the family group caused him distress: his mother's sister, *tante* Séraphie, a sharp-tongued bigoted unmarried woman who ruled over the household. When she died, at still a fairly young age, the boy fell to his knees and thanked God. There is not much doubt that Séraphie was responsible for some of Stendhal's impulses of distrust and violence.

Abbé Raillane was hired by Chérubin Beyle as a private tutor for his son. The purpose of this appointment was to teach the boy manners and to make him respectful of conventions and authority. In the eyes of Henri, the priest was a narrow-minded tyrant who became a hateful presence in the house and who caused the boy to break definitively with his father and with the Church. Under the oppressive treatment, which he doubtless exaggerated, of his father, of Séraphie and of Abbé Raillane, Henri Beyle grew into a boy whose nature was strongly individualistic, disrespectful and impulsive. The three tyrants represented not only the bourgeoisie of Grenoble he learned to loathe, but also humanity at large. At war with his family and without friends—he claimed he was never allowed to play with other boys—whatever sentimentality, whatever feelings of affection were in Henri Beyle were repressed during his childhood. Because of a misdeed for which he was punished in the presence of all the family, he turned against his grandfather Gagnon.

The six years that elapsed between his mother's death in November 1790 and the beginning of his studies in the Ecole Centrale de Grenoble in November 1796 were years of suffering more than years of happiness for the boy when, in revolt against his family environment, he developed a spirit of independence, a precocious spirit of curiosity, a growing sense of psychic and physical needs. He could be moved to tears by the sound of bells and elated by the slightest attention from his uncle Romain Gagnon, but he learned to repress most expressions of such feelings while savoring them inwardly in order to carry on a secret existence in direct contrast with the fatuous dull routine life he was forced to live in the house on the rue des Vieux-Jésuites where he had been born. The boy's sensitivity was real and deep. Years after the first sentimental dramas, when he wrote about them in *Henry Brulard,* he relived the emotions and remembered their intensity. *Le coeur me bat encore en écrivant ceci, trente-six ans après.*

There was almost no outlet in the way of exercise or sports, no horseback riding, no hunting, which would have been normal pastimes for a boy growing up in the Dauphiné and in Henri Beyle's social milieu. He was quite literally cloistered, overly protected, rigorously isolated from all normal activities and encounters that would have hardened him and probably made him into something not a writer. All extrovert activity was replaced by daydreaming, by a taste for introversion and meditation that became habits and attitudes that lasted throughout his life. He learned early to nurture that sensitiveness and vanity from which he suffered all his life. Before Byronism struck France, Henri Beyle was a youthful Byronic hero whose romantic nature was developed by his longing for happiness. In his later years such a formula was the very basis of his ethical system.

The boy became aware of what the beauty of nature could mean for him during the summer of 1791, which he spent with his newly married uncle Romain Gagnon in Les Echelles. Instinctively he was romantic in his love for nature. His early attraction to women, to his mother, to his aunt, in Les Echelles, for example, was more purely physical. Precociously and sensuously Henri Beyle was attracted to all women he met.

At the age of twelve or thirteen, he was writing comedies, modeled more on Destouches than on Molière. At ten, he had read *Manon Lescaut* and *La Nouvelle Héloïse.* He had little interest in Racine and Corneille, except for *Le Cid,* of which he had seen a performance with his uncle Romain. He had read some of the forbidden books: *Les Contes* of La Fontaine, for example, and *Les Liaisons Dangereuses.* Whereas most boys pass through this period of reading when their imagination and senses are enflamed by forbidden books read secretly, Beyle never ceased being that kind of reader. He never ceased being the child and the adolescent, the romantic, in the French sense of *romanesque,* who lives imaginatively more than realistically, who lives on the stimulation of his senses and the mysterious power of his fantasies. The writer, and especially the kind of writer Stendhal was to become, has to remain the child who peoples his mind with such persistent phantoms that they become real and have to be given a life of their own.

Between thirteen and fourteen Henri Beyle began his studies at the Ecole Centrale de Grenoble, a type of school, founded by law the fourth year of the First Republic in 1795, with a broader scope of studies than the program offered by the French *lycée*. This marked the boy's first separation from his family, the first experience of freedom, which quickly turned into disappointment and general bewilderment.

The subjects studied were history, mathematics, physics, chemistry, a special kind of analytical grammar, modern languages, drawing, literature. Henri was an excellent pupil, winning prizes in literature and mathematics. His literature teacher emphasized the classics of the seventeenth century, but also added the reading of such figures as Voltaire and Shakespeare. It was he who introduced Beyle to Locke, Condillac and Helvétius. Mathematics satisfied his need for precision and rigor, and he was to continue reading Saint-Simon and Shakespeare all his life. He was a fairly fat boy and was jokingly called by his companions, who on the whole did not like him very much, *la tour ambulante*. He made a few friends, however, among the most serious of the students. There were episodes that upset the routine of the few years at Centrale, such as a duel and the shooting of a sign in the middle of the Place Grenette.

As early as fifteen, love was an all-important problem, and he tended to conceal other less important matters in order to continue with his amorous dreams. He quite literally lusted after all women, young and old, who entered his life. He was perhaps sixteen, when he fell in love with a young actress in the Théâtre de Grenoble, Mlle. Cubly. Because this Virginie sang, Henri tried to learn music and study singing, the violin and the clarinet. He had no particular endowments for music. This early infatuation remained silent. He never dared approach Mlle. Cubly, and when she left Grenoble in 1798, he stopped going to the theater.

He tells of one day in the classroom, looking out over the ramparts and plain and beyond them to the hills, the Dauphiné Alps, and feeling intensely the beauty of the landscape. Beyle's passion for such landscapes is present throughout his writing.

Such was his success at the Ecole Centrale, especially in mathematics, that in the last year of the century his teachers prevailed upon his father to allow the boy to go to Paris, to compete in the examination for L'Ecole Polytechnique, the prestige of which was as high then as it is today. He had counted, even a few years earlier, on his ability in mathematics to get him out of Grenoble. This indeed was the case. In November 1799 he climbed into the coach that was to take him to Paris, after hearing a strange farewell speech from his Uncle Romain. Briefly put, Romain Gagnon warned him not to lay too much hope on his skill as mathematician and to remember that a man makes his way in life by means of a woman. But you are ugly, *tu es laid*, Romain said to Henri, and if you hope to succeed, make love within twenty-four hours to some woman, even if she is a chamber maid!

In *Vie de Henry Brulard*, Stendhal explains by the mysterious word *espagnolisme* the way in which he reacted against his education, his family and his first torment of love. He calls *espagnolisme* the feeling of disgust for everything that is low and commonplace, a scorn for money and commerce. It is a feeling comparable to the sense of honor that *Le Cid* illustrates. It is highly probable that Stendhal's *espagnolisme* was quite simply a reaction against the constraining influences and ideas of his family, of their bourgeois judgments and habits. He was seventeen on reaching Paris. His head seemed too large for his body at that time. His knowledge of the world was limited to what he had read in novels, and it was going to be difficult for him to adjust to the real world of every day.

First, at the Hôtel de Bourgogne, he looked up students of Polytechnique who had come from Grenoble the year before. For lodging, he chose a modest room on the rue du Bac, and then paid his respects to Noël Daru, a first cousin of Dr. Gagnon. When, after a few weeks of miserable exist-ence in Paris, Beyle fell seriously ill with a stomach ailment, Noël Daru had him consult an eminent doctor and gave him a room in his own house on the rue de Lille.

The Daru household did not in the least represent what Beyle hoped for in Paris society. Noël Daru, the father, was a stern gentleman who treated his provincial cousin as if he were an idler. His older son Pierre, destined to be one day the *intendant général* of Napoleon's army, was completely absorbed by his position in the war ministry. The younger son, Martial, was more outgoing and affectionate, but his friendship with Henri really began a few years later, and he never became the close friend that Henri needed. The women of the family, Mme. Daru and her married daugh-ters, showed only a minimum politeness to Beyle. In their presence he felt ill-at-ease and inferior. In the first letter Noël Daru dictated to Beyle, the young man misspelled the simple word *cela* by adding an *l* (*cella*). How could a young writer and humanist, with such spelling habits, have won school prizes in Grenoble? The anecdote of *cella* will be reproduced in *Le Rouge et le Noir*.

Abruptly one day, M. Daru announced that Pierre had found for his cousin a modest secretarial position with the war office. Disillusioned with this work and with his failure to secure a promotion, three months later, in May 1800, Henri Beyle crossed the Alps to join the reserve army. He reached Milan the day after the victory of Marengo. There he became soldier, first a *maréchal-des-logis,* and then a *sous-lieutenant de dragons.*

From the beginning Milan appeared to him a place of enchantment. The few months he spent there in 1800 were some of the happiest of his life. Between 1800 and 1821 he dreamed uninterruptedly of living in Milan. He described the Milanese enthusiasm over the arrival of the French army (and this he doubtless exaggerated according to his most painstaking biographer Paul Arbalet). He wrote of the magnificent music and the mediocre actors at La Scala. He praised the beauty of several Milanese ladies, especially of one Angela Pietragrua, the mistress of his office mate Joinville. This Angela had been an intimate friend of the painter Gros. Beyle fell in love with her immediately and stayed in love for some time. Eleven years later he became her lover.

His first sexual experience occurred soon after his arrival in Milan, and left him with a venereal disease he had to treat intermittently the rest of his life. Beyle claimed he had no precise memory of the event or the accompanying circumstances. This is difficult to believe because for most young men, and especially for the highly sensitive and romantic nature of a Henri Beyle, the initiation to sex is memorable. Stendhal's life story is far less accurate than that of his heroes.

But this early misadventure did not disgust Beyle with Milan and with Italian women. As he languished over his love for Angela, while at the same time attending performances at La Scala and gatherings at the Casino, he developed a form of love, a sensitivity to love that were to be characteristic of his life. It was a longing for love, a romantic conception of happiness that was melancholic and passionate, but silently passionate. In his feelings of love for Angela Pietragrua, he saw the signs of his capacity for emotional attachment. Ten years later when he comments on the year 1800 in Milan, Stendhal sees himself as Cherubino, the Beaumarchais character of a lovesick boy who blushes when a woman passes by, who trembles at such words as "love" and "voluptuousness."

Beyle's military career was a means to other careers. He began keeping his *Journal* on April 18, 1801, and it is difficult to believe that he belonged to the sixth regiment of the dragons, while at the same time he was concerned with Italian lessons, fencing lessons, horseback riding, plays and operas, and with constant preoccupations over women—over how to please them and hold them, to intrigue them and solicit their favors. Stendhal will use his knowledge of military life in his writing, but in the formation of his character it seems to have counted very little. He spent eighteen months of campaign fighting without ever really being a soldier. He was not a coward, but his bravery was a function and not an enthusiasm.

During the eighteen months of active military service, the only documents on Beyle's mind and activity are his letters to his sister Pauline and his *Journal*. It is clear from such sources that he had no inclination toward the discomforts of military life. The writer's life was the temptation, with all its attendant satisfactions of success. The somewhat enforced military career was perhaps useful in making more clear and more tempting the vocation of writer. By the end of 1801 he had made up his mind to resign from the army.

The uniform of dragon had not been important for Beyle, but the eighteen months in Italy had been of extreme importance. There he learned that beauty is attainable, that romantic love does exist and that social pleasures are possible for him. He had been entranced by the lakes and mountains of Bergamo, by the operas and ballets of La Scala, by the rather easy fun-loving social life of Milan to which he had been introduced by Martial Daru and Joinville, by the Lombard beauty of Angela Pietragrua. When he left Milan for three months in Grenoble, and then for Paris, with the determination to succeed, he meant by such a word as "succeed" the ability to make love, to write and to secure for himself a high place in that social world that he enjoyed. Each of these envied roles: amorous, scriptorial and worldly he knew to be of a more arduous kind of campaigning than that he had just experienced in Napoleon's army.

Henri Beyle was far from being the first provincial at the age of twenty to come to Paris in search of pleasure and success. In the wake of the Revolution, conditions were supposed to be more democratic for such young men. Personal merit was supposed to count more than birth. Young men of Beyle's generation were conscious of their rights, aware of the new dogma of equality, eager to prove themselves and seize what they could of the national and social heritage.

Beyle was quite different from the typical Balzac hero whose triumphs and failures were to be so brilliantly recorded in the case histories of Lucien de Rubempré, Eugène de Rastignac, Horace Bianchon and a host of others. His ambition was far more centered on his sensibility, on the development and power of his perceptiveness, than on any worldly ambition. On this second trip to Paris, he had no family name of importance, no wealth and no rank that might permit him to move in those social circles where he wished to be. The only home to which he had easy access was that of the Darus who held the kind of salon that was to be allied with Napoleon's court.

At the age of twenty, on his return to Paris, Beyle represented for the Darus the poor relative. For others, he represented, for the most part, the provincial intruder. He used every possible means to make a place for himself, and he succeeded tolerably well. The younger Daru, Martial, had begun by this time to treat Henri Beyle as a companion. Literature was Beyle's constant preoccupation, and the theater was that aspect of literature that attracted him the most forcibly. He would become a poet in the theater, he would replace Molière as the new poet of comedies. His great social encounters were literary. He was able to see, for example, Mme. de Staël, and he was received in the most exclusive salon of Paris, that of Mme. Récamier. But he was poor, and his impoverishment was a source of irritation and humiliation all during this second period in Paris. To study, he needed books, and to appear in society, he needed clothes and spending money.

Beyle's love escapades were on the whole imaginary. He tried to explain his timidity and awkwardness in courtship by his penuriousness. This might be questioned. Perhaps he preferred mental love affairs. At times everything seemed to count against him: his Grenoble accent, his far from handsome physical appearance, his sense of inferiority. With Martial Daru, elegant, finely mannered, suave, he felt as Julien Sorel will feel in the presence of Norbert de la Mole. Beyle was tormented by what he considered his speech deficiencies, his inability to carry on a conversation, to reply wittily, to pick up an argument and carry it through. He was ashamed of his frequent demonstrations of surprise. He knew that the Parisian lad of his age never demonstrated surprise over anything.

His vanity was always being hurt, and therefore he never seemed able to reach that carefreeness of manner, that ease of behavior and speech he envied so much in others. Like a Prufrock of the nineteenth century, he felt that all eyes were staring at him and seeing through him or pinning him to the wall. He was too inexperienced to realize that most men were too self-centered to pay any attention to him in the first place. He argued with himself in his journal and pleaded with himself to be more natural in the presence of others. That would be the only way by which to please them. He often returned in his personal writings to the problem of why he was hurt so easily, or why the simple inflection of a word or an insignificant gesture could transport him to happiness or to despair.

The reality of his encounters in the social world, which usually turned out to be so distasteful and so unsatisfactory that he would launch into a tirade of self-deprecation, was the opposite of the life he imagined in his dreams and read about in books. There, valued friendship would accompany success in love and success in his vocation of writer. Such contradictions and such scruples will characterize and torment Julien Sorel. Of course, the man's pride is always close at hand, both Beyle's and Julien Sorel's, to reassure him that he is superior and that the world of men about him is vulgar and platitudinous. It is not too difficult for him to argue with himself that such a temperament as he possesses must by its very nature, by its very uniqueness, remain apart from other men. He was destined to be different and to be alone.

Such a conviction will help transform Henri Beyle into Stendhal, to convert the bourgeois *arriviste* from Grenoble into the writer. His very vacillation between extreme distrust of self and extreme exaltation of self is both a method

for the writer and the source for a writer's vision. The difficult years in Paris, when he felt neglected by those he
wanted to befriend and ludicrous in his behavior, developed in Henri Beyle traits of childishness he was never to
dispell. With the passing of years he did become more manly
and more cynical, but the suffering child in him never
disappeared and it was beyond doubt that part of his temperament that fostered the writer. His memories of dissatisfac-
tions and humiliations were the deepest. These were the
experiences that were to shape his protagonists. In his forties
Stendhal could easily remember Henri Beyle at twenty.

The years 1803–1805 in Paris were marked by a love affair
with a young girl of his own age, Victorine Mounier, whom
he saw infrequently. It was a typical case of imaginary and
imaginative love-making that did not last long. During the
same year Beyle's reading and study were more important,
especially his reading of such authors as Helvétius and Destutt de Tracy who were to help formulate his ideology and
his *beylisme*. At the same time the theater appealed to him
more and more forcibly. He studied with well-known diction teachers in order to correct his Grenoble accent. He
learned the role of Oreste in *Andromaque* and tried to meet
some of the great actors of the day, even Talma himself.
He took part in salon theatrical performances and persisted
in trying to write comedies and projects for comedies.
Throughout all these efforts, which were without success,
Beyle enjoyed, with an almost adolescent glee, the feminine
encounters in the salons and in the diction classes.

It was there he met, in 1804, an actress three years older
than himself, with whom he fell in love. Mélanie Guilbert
was usually called Louason. In letters to Pauline, her
brother described Mélanie's Greek features and blue eyes
and graceful body. The infatuation was strong enough to

make him follow her to Marseille where she was to act in the Grand Théâtre. This was in 1805.

The theatrical enterprise was a failure for Louason, who soon returned to Paris. In his journal, Beyle noted down all the stages of disappointment with Mélanie, especially with the limitations of her mind. He analyzed his sense of liberation when she left Marseille and marveled at the sense of dryness in him after the fullness of feeling and exaltation he had at one time experienced. He wondered whether happiness would always be in a place where he was not.

After the Marseille interlude, Henri Beyle's life changed quite drastically. Thanks to the intervention of Pierre Daru, he was appointed *adjoint provisoire* in the war office (*Commissaire des Guerres*) and soon held the post officially. He was present at Napoleon's entrance into Berlin in October 1806. For two years, stationed principally in Brunswick, he studied German with no enthusiasm and manifested very little interest in German literature and philosophy.

He profited from the prestige of his cousins the Darus and enjoyed Brunswick social life. French was spoken in that world that remembered Voltaire's visit to Frederick II and Rivarol's visit to the Berlin Academy. By this time, Beyle had lost some of his social timidity and felt at ease in German society. There were dinner parties, balls, evenings spent playing cards or giving play readings. He often went hunting (he was a good pistol shot) and enjoyed drinking with his friends at an inn at the edge of the forest, the *Chasseur vert* (*zum grünen Jäger*), which Stendhal will utilize in *Lucien Leuwen*.

He fell in love with the youngest daughter of Major-General von Griesheim, Wilhelmine, who was called "Minette" by her friends. The episode was a flaring up and rather swift dying out of passion. Beyle could not bring himself to contemplate marriage, and Wilhelmine did not wish to be his mistress. Once again, he savored the pleasures of being in love and did not suffer too much when the episode was over. Minette represented for him the simple German virtues. The affair was an idyl and it brought satisfaction and exaltation to one side at least of Beyle's nature. Many years later he referred to Minette de Griesheim as the major love affair of his life.

He continued his reading of Tracy and Helvétius. He cultivated a taste for Mozart and sent his sister the score of *Don Giovanni.* He began preferring Mozart to Cimarosa whose music he had liked so much in Italy. All these experiences—amatory, intellectual and aesthetic—were changing the awkward Grenoble bourgeois into a French dandy.

But he returned to the active army and in 1809 followed the French army marching against Austria. He spent six months in Vienna where he attended Haydn's funeral. During the next few years he saw, not the battles of Napoleon, but the aftermath of the battles, the scenes of horror on the battlefields, the wounded in crowded hospitals, violent contrasts of a beautiful landscape and decomposing bodies scattered throughout the landscape and particularly the still-burning fires of entire villages.

A somewhat mysterious intimacy with Pierre Daru's wife developed in 1809 and 1810. During the months of 1810 that he spent in Paris, Beyle lived as a dandy, enjoying the theater, society and the beauty of various women he encountered there. This was probably the happiest period of his life. He held a position in the Imperial Court, he felt himself more a Parisian than a provincial. He felt he was accomplishing his goals at precisely the moment when a violent turn in history, the fall of Napoleon, upset his plans and hopes.

From 1812 on, Milan became more than ever his favorite
city. He admired the music the city offered. There, he fell in
love with Métilde Dembowska. There, he participated with
considerable ease and naturalness in the social life. The epitaph that he himself devised is proof of his attachment to
Milan, to the freedom the city afforded him, to the sense
that he was a man of some importance there. His first book,
written in 1814, *Vies de Haydn, de Mozart et de Métastase,*
did not solve the question of what kind of writing he should
do. Should he be a musicologist, or an art critic, or a literary
critic? Beyle was happier in Milan during his thirties than
he had ever been in Paris, but he longed for the prestige
of Paris, he longed to be a famous man in the capital of his
own country.

The epitaph, in its complete form, read:

> *Arrigo Beyle*
> *Milanese*
> *Visse, scrisse, amò.*
> *Quest'anima*
> *Adorava*
> *Cimarosa, Mozart e Shakespeare*
> *Morì di anni . . .*
> *il . . . 18 . . .*

(Henri Beyle, of Milan, lived, wrote and loved. This soul
worshipped Cimarosa, Mozart and Shakespeare. He died at
the age of . . . in 18 . . .)

When, for the publication of *Rome, Naples et Florence*
in 1817, he used the pseudonym of M. de Stendhal, bor-
rowed from the name of a German city, life took on for
him a new glamor he was to lose and then recover in successive moments of depression and exaltation.

It would be difficult to overestimate the effect of Métilde
Dembowska on Beyle. She was a magnificent sad woman

who, without loving or pitying Beyle, inspired him with an understanding of love that will find its way into *De l'Amour* and into such major works as *Le Rouge et le Noir*, *Lucien Leuwen* and *La Chartreuse de Parme*. When, in 1825, he learned of the premature death of Métilde, he recorded it in his copy of *De l'Amour*, with the inscription in English: "Death of the author." At seventeen, Métilde had married a Polish officer Jean Dembowski, much older than she, who became a general in Napoleon's army. There were two sons. Dembowski suspected his wife of being the mistress of the Italian poet Ugo Foscolo. Beyle met her ten years after this presumed affair with Foscolo, and because of the scandal, which had circulated in Milan, believed he might win her too. She never gave herself to Beyle. Her beauty was for him a "promise of happiness" (*promesse de bonheur*). He compared his feelings for her to that form of love sung of by the poets of the *dolce stil nuovo*. When he saw her one day in the street at a distance, the beating of his heart reminded him of a comparable scene in Dante's *Vita Nuova*. Métilde was one further example in Stendhal's life of a great passion that remained in the state of sentimentality.

When he returned to Paris, in 1821, he was thirty-eight years old. He led there a limited social life, and published during the next nine years six books: *De l'Amour*, *Racine et Shakespeare*, *Vie de Rossini*, *Armance*, *Promenades dans Rome* and *Le Rouge et le Noir*. Although he was writing more, and although his name was beginning to be known in intellectual circles, his way of life did not change very much during the nine years. In 1830 he became a consul in the service of Louis-Philippe and was appointed first at Trieste and then at Città Vecchia, close to Rome. He was bored by everything in Città Vecchia, by the pettinesses connected with his profession and by the dullness of the city. It was there he probably wrote most of *La Chartreuse de Parme* and *Les Chroniques italiennes*.

Beyle discovered that the one way to survive in Città Vecchia was to spend five days out of every seven in Rome. During the last ten years of his life he gradually became a lover of Rome (*romano*) after being a *milanese*. As long as he remained a civil servant (*fonctionnaire*), he refrained from publishing. But he wrote extensively: his *Souvenirs d'égotisme,* the novel *Lucien Leuwen,* which he never completed, his very detailed autobiography, *Vie de Henry Brulard,* in which he did not go beyond his adolescence. *Lamiel,* his last attempt at writing a novel, was composed between 1839 and 1842. During his constant contact with Rome, he kept planning to rewrite and enlarge his *Promenades dans Rome*. All aspects of the "eternal city" fascinated him: the social habits, the arts, Roman chronicles and memoirs. He had little inclination for reading Roman history. Cellini's *Vita* and the works of the short story writers (the *novellieri*) were more appealing. This study grew into one of Stendhal's least studied books and which may in time occupy a more important place than it does today: *Les Chroniques italiennes* of 1839. In his remarks about Italian social classes, Beyle's admiration went decidedly to the masses, to *le peuple italien,* for the traits he admired: their simplicity, their innate intelligence and intuitive feelings about art, their talent for satire.

He manifested no interest in the Roman Church, no interest in spiritual problems or mysticism. Whenever Stendhal's egotism helped him to reach a rather profound knowledge of the ego, he had nothing in him, no drive or no curiosity, that might be called the aspirations of a theologian. Neither did he have any of the typically Voltairian traits: no feelings of deliberate hate or impiety in terms of the Church. He was not sensitive to the spirituality of Catholicism, but he admired the political action of the great popes. For him the Roman Church was an extraordinary empire, an unusually competent political system.

Despite bad health, he led an active social life, at the famous café Greco, where artists and writers mingled, and at the Caetani palace on the via delle Botteghe Oscure, where the principessa Caetani was a generous patroness of intellectuals and artists. His friendship for Roman ladies usually turned into something more fervent than friendship (into what the French call *amitié amoureuse*) and something just a bit less than a real liaison. When, in 1837, he spent several months of leave in Paris, he missed his Roman life. In a marginal note on one of his manuscripts, he transposed the word *Roma* into its anagram *Amore*.

As Stendhal grew older—in 1840 he was fifty-seven, and had only two years longer to live—he felt more and more the sensation of watching himself live than actually living. He maintained a certain degree of curiosity about life even if the desire to live had markedly diminished. He dreamed of love more than ever before and indulged in memories of affairs that had been almost successful. The ghosts of innumerable feminine figures quite literally obsessed him at the time when, in the space of fifty-two days, he wrote *La Chartreuse de Parme*. The persistent sadness in Stendhal— only a bit more apparent in his last years than in his earlier years—seemed to come from his incapacity to make a woman deliriously totally happy. At every age Stendhal was the adloescent, loving love, fearful of not being attractive to women and not being sexually capable of satisfying them. Far more than most men, Stendhal pursued the image of happiness in love throughout his life, without ever trying to understand, or at least to acknowledge to himself, why he was implacably unsuccessful. In more than one place in his writings, at the end of his life, Stendhal confessed to a lack of self-knowledge—*je ne me connais pas moi-même*—and interpreted this as the basic reason for his unhappiness and for his defeats: . . . *et c'est ce qui, quand j'y pense, me désole.*

When his regrets began to outnumber his desires, Stendhal realized he was approaching the end of his life, and at that time his consolation came from a conviction that posterity would honor him, that he would grow into himself after his death. He lived on that conviction Mallarmé was to designate as the fate of Poe and of any artist: *Tel qu'en lui-même enfin l'éternité le change.* This survival, by which the man, after his death, is transformed uniquely into the artist, was the only kind in which Stendhal could believe. Just before his death, he had the joy of reading Balzac's glowing article on *La Chartreuse de Parme.* This praise was the first indication of what "the happy few" were to propagate in the years to come when Henri Beyle had definitively grown into Stendhal.

The memories at the end of the life that had remained the most steadfast in his mind were not those of ideas or political events or wars. They were the visual memories of a woman he had once loved, of her smile, of an expression on her face. He was unable to make a moral estimate, do a moral stocktaking of himself, and decided that the balance sheet of that ego he had so carefully analyzed all his life was best expressed in his strong sentiments of pleasure and pain, of desire and of dislike.

The first attack of, presumably, apoplexy came in March 1841. From then on, Stendhal suffered intermittently from aphasia, from brief spells of a loss of the power of speech. This very specific introduction to death elicited no blas-

phemy and no arch whimpering or sentimentality. His sense
of resignation was noble. It was both rational and instinctive. It is possible that the last words he wrote were a three-
line letter to his cousin Romain Colomb on June 9, 1841,
which described his two dogs, a black spaniel and a light
brown "lupetto." "I was sad at having nothing to love,"
were the last words: *J'étais triste de n'avoir rien à aimer.* A
pathetic irony for the man who had created such passionate
heroines as Mathilde de la Mole and La Sanseverina and
such lovers as Julien and Fabrice. He hoped his death
would be swift and that he would be spared old age, and
he hoped also that he might leave Italy and return home to
France. His official leave of absence did come, and he set
out for France on October 11, 1841, with the knowledge
that he would never again return to Rome.

Five months later, in March 1842, in Paris, on the rue
des Capucines, Beyle collapsed under a massive stroke and
died a few hours later in his hotel room at the age of fifty-
nine. A funeral service was celebrated in the Eglise de
l'Assomption. Three friends accompanied the body to the
Cimetière Montmartre: Romain Colomb, Abraham Con-
stantin and Prosper Mérimée.

During the three weeks that preceded his death, Stendhal
had worked hard on his writing. He corrected the second
edition of *La Chartreuse de Parme*, wrote a chapter of
Lamiel and worked on the story *Suora Scolastica.* At that
time he was seriously considering submitting his name as
a candidate to the Académie Française.

His cousin Colomb and his sister Pauline were in Paris
when he died, and they made the arrangements for the
church funeral, a favor that Beyle himself would probably
not have solicited. A monument, with the desired inscription filled in, was placed at the grave:

Arrigo Beyle
Milanese
Scrisse
Amò
Visse
An. LTX.M.II.
Morì LLXXIII *Marzo*
M.D. CCCXLII

Beyle had felt himself a Milanese during the years in Paris when he was ill at ease there and maladjusted to French social life. But it was in Paris that he wrote *Le Rouge et le Noir*. He lived in Milan only six years and after that period found the city less to his liking. At the end of his life he had become an authentic Parisian. Even if Italy did count tremendously in the personality of Stendhal, to have himself called a Milanese on the gravestone in the Cimetière Montmartre was an error, explained somewhat by that type of whim or fancy of which the writer gave countless instances throughout his life.

The many neuroses from which Stendhal suffered would cause him to be classified by a psychiatrist today as paranoid. All of the classic elements of the paranoid were in Stendhal: his very particular type of mind and mental outlook where pride dominated, with a large degree of irritability or susceptibility. The lack of discipline in his nature was translated into a strong dislike for authority, a scorn for the ordinary person and for those people whose position in life represented some kind of power or direction. The paranoiac needs to feel respected. In order to represent to himself and to others the dubious fact that he is respected, he will go as far as lying about the signs of this respect. The fundamental trait of the paranoiac is the conviction that he is persecuted, and to himself especially, but to others also, he will magnify and misinterpret all the details that justify his sense of being persecuted. Everything makes sense in the stories of a paranoid, although no one detail is rigorously true.

The paranoiac temperament has an extraordinary range. The same degree of pride and the same tendency to prevarication can exist in sufferers from paranoia who are impossible in the social sense and those who are thoroughly charming. The paranoid Henri Beyle, possessing a very high intelligence, was a man of great charm who delighted and attracted almost all those he approached. Even in his paranoiac confessions, both oral and written, Beyle's astuteness and keen intelligence kept him from going too far and thus bewildering his companion and his future readers. This hypothetical analysis is based on the personal writings of Stendhal, where he wrote down directly so much of what passed through his mind: his letters, his *Journal,* his *Souvenirs d'égotisme,* his *Vie de Henry Brulard.* If he had not been the compulsive writer that he was, unable not to write, our understanding of Stendhal and our interpretations of his major books would be very different.

Biographer after biographer, critic after critic have used excessively the word failure in characterizing every aspect of Beyle's character and vocation. Failure as a lover has been the favorite tag. With our greater understanding today of paranoia, we can wonder if such a judgment or such a qualification has much meaning. Even if we grant that love is lied about more than any other human experience, it would seem that Beyle had quite an honorable list of mistresses. By his intimate friends, he was looked upon as a man at least mildly successful in his amorous adventures. At the end of his life, when he made marriage proposals to a few women, he was refused; but it is fairly clear that he did not propose with the ardor of a man who really wanted what he was asking for. He was, to repeat the English cliché, a confirmed bachelor. (The French give the phrase a more elegant turn when they say *un célibataire de vocation*.) The life of a bachelor was characteristic of so many major French writers of the nineteenth century, in addition to Stendhal, that it could easily be looked upon as a "vocation": Baudelaire, Mérimée, Nerval, Sainte-Beuve, Flaubert (and Balzac until a few months before his death). No one of these men, with the possible exception of Baudelaire, has ever been accused of being a failure as a lover.

To call Beyle a failure in his military career is tantamount to denying his determination to resign from the army (where he might have risen to the highest rank had he persevered) in order to become a writer. If Napoleon had not fallen, Beyle's diplomatic career might well have flourished more than it did. The post at Cività Vecchia, from which he was so often absent, demanded very little of his attention.

The third and most serious accusation of failure concerns Stendhal's career of writer. Often this accusation is based upon the fact that he never became a member of the Académie Française! This would be as risky a criterion to apply as that of monetary returns from books published during the lifetime of a writer. Today at least two or three of France's outstanding writers are not members of the Academy: Sartre, Malraux, Julien Green. The acknowledgment or lack of acknowledgment of widespread critical favor during the writer's lifetime is also an unsound criterion. All such criteria have been used to classify Stendhal as a *raté*. But Stendhal in his own lifetime had attracted the attention and elicited the admiration of such writers as George Sand and Balzac, of Mérimée and Alfred de Musset. Sainte-Beuve's lack of appreciation of Stendhal has often been cited. But Sainte-Beuve's taste and literary judgment were far from being sound, especially in terms of his contemporaries. Many years later, Marcel Proust was to denounce Sainte-Beuve for his failure to understand the greatness of those three writers he considered the most important in the nineteenth century: Baudelaire, Nerval and Stendhal, all of whom Sainte-Beuve had known personally.

What counts today is Stendhal's power as a writer, the power by which, even on pages where he reveals irritating personal idiosyncrasies, he holds an ever-increasing public of readers with the way he enunciates an idea or delineates some aspect of truth in the turn of a conversation, in some simply stated and unexpected observation. The pleasure he still gives, especially to that type of reader who has read a great deal, is in the form of a lesson where Stendhal the writer teaches his reader not to take himself too seriously and even not to take the writer too seriously. Stendhal's wisdom, in a word, is his understanding of life, his skill at making his reader aware of the uncertainties of life, of the insecurities of dogmas, of the relative importance of those moments in life judged to be important, of the ever-changing quality of pleasure. The reader's pleasure in Stendhal is the unaffected way in which such revelations are made to him.

The writings of Stendhal are an extraordinarily accurate reflection of his personality and of his thought that combined countless paradoxical conflicts and desires. But these very contradictions made of Stendhal the writer a representative man in the sense that Emerson makes of such a figure as, for example, Montaigne. Stendhal, the skeptic in everything that relates to philosophical or theological absolutism, and Stendhal, the lover of that willed forcefulness in man he called "energy," the deployment of *espagnolisme,* are behind those moments in his work that call forth in the reader a feeling of sympathy for the writer's understanding of foibles and dreams and fantasies and a feeling of respect for man who—despite foibles, dreams and fantasies—is able to achieve lasting monuments of art.

One can have many reservations about the style of Stendhal's writing when contrasting it with the style of a Flaubert or of a Proust. It is the style of an able conversationalist who, when he writes, gives the impression of talking out loud to himself. But this written conversation carried on with himself is never tiresome, never flat. The improvisations follow one another—as they would in a real conversation—wittily, intelligently, always without rhetorical flourish or ornamentation. From scene to scene in the novels, there may be an arbitrariness of structure, an unlikelihood, an awkwardness in transitions, but within every scene, the tone of the conversation is so vibrant, so sincere, that the reader follows it and forgets the general effect of the structure. The greatest guarantee of all for a continuing interest in the books of Stendhal is that they were written by a man who loved social intercourse, who loved women as those beings occupying the center of social intercourse, and who, quite simply, loved life.

The circumstances of Stendhal's death might easily be interpreted as symbolic of his life, of the unusual life story of a man who, while cherishing the traditional recipes for happiness in the family and society, never followed them for himself, or was unable to follow them. The secrecy of Octave's life in *Armance* is not unlike the secretiveness of Stendhal's life, although the reasons for the secretiveness may be different. (One is often inclined to believe that they might have been quite similar.)

Alone in Paris, on the rue Neuve-des-Petits-Champs

(called today the rue des Capucines), almost at the door of
the ministry of foreign affairs and close to the Place Ven-
dôme, apoplexy struck him down, and a few hours later he
died in his hotel room. Stendhal never had a permanent
address, nor a permanent profession. He had no home, no
children, and, we can almost say, no mistress. Those love
affairs that had some duration were unhappy. They survived
in his imagination rather than in his life.

It would be too facile, and indeed inaccurate, to conclude
that this was the kind of life he wanted. His nature craved
intimacy. This was a fact too often expressed in his writings
to overlook. Beyle's relationship with his sister Pauline was
significant in this respect. His strong affection for her began
early, in contrast with his hatred for Séraphie and Séraphie's
persecutions. The many letters he wrote to Pauline from
Paris, from Marseille, from Germany prove that she was his
confidante. The tone he used in writing to Pauline was more
intimate than the tone of his personal journals. His part
was that of a Platonic lover who wanted to shape her life.
He often spoke of finding for her in Paris a suitable husband, and then spending the rest of his life close by and
thereby participating in his sister's married life. This was
not realized. Pauline married a stolid citizen of Grenoble in
1808, and from then on the brother's letters diminished in
number, and the intimate tone of the letters changed, as if
Beyle realized they would be read by two people.

After Pauline's marriage, Beyle had quite literally no
family. More than most men, he strove to maintain friendships, and even those friendships that went back to his
childhood. According to all the documents that are acces-
sible, his friends showed little or no real sympathy for
Beyle and no comprehension of his nature. The death
notice, drawn up by Romain Colomb, who had known him

all his life, was as lacking in comprehension as Mérimée's notes on his friend entitled *H. B.* Mérimée was one of those friends whom Beyle saw frequently in meetings that were a habit. Beyle felt very much alone in such gatherings where familiarity and a ribald joviality reigned and where he was often pained by a critical tone and even a tone of malice.

The salons were somewhat different for Beyle, because there women were present, but he was never the center, never the honored guest of any salon. He attended them intermittently, and when he ceased going to a salon, it was usually with a feeling of deep disappointment and even bitterness. His social life in Italy was easier, but more superficial. He was more relaxed there, but even in Milan and Rome he did not find the ideal social life he longed to know. And yet, society never took first place in Beyle's life. From the beginning, he knew what it was and judged it as a diversion that was to be added to the fuller and more meaningful part of his life. It would be fair to say that Beyle remained more envious of social life than a participant in it. His ceaseless moving about from city to city, from country to country, in itself forced him into a solitude that he both wanted and dreaded. His vagabond life was spent without any enduring attachment to a human being or to a place. His ever-changing social life attracted him, diverted him but never altered his emotions and his convictions. At a very early age, Beyle's sentiments, emotions and reactions were the same that they were to be at the time of his death. He was a fervent observer of life wherever he lived, but he was unaffected by it. He preserved and protected his original sensibility through the years. He never assumed those multiple responsibilities of marriage, of paternity and of a career that inevitably change a young man into an older man and end by clouding and eradicating the dreams and ideals and vibrant reactions of a young man. As in the case of Marcel Proust, with whom Stendhal has much more in common than has ever been pointed out, the present was composed of the past.

The fundamental life of Beyle, the biography of his feelings and thoughts and fantasies, is in each of his novels he signed Stendhal. These novels narrate the same story of the same young man. They are compositions about Henri Beyle's fantasies, richly documented, placed in a variety of settings, each evocative of a different world, but each the same story of a young man who is unable or who refuses to grow into adulthood. Each book of Stendhal is the account of a young man's charm that attracts the people around him or instills envy in those who are attracted in a hostile way. One forgives a youth every misdemeanor if he remains attractive, spontaneous in his reactions, capricious. One forgives him everything provided he is either the incipient seducer or a real seducer. A seduction carried out at the age of twenty bears a mystical element of grace in that it represents both an initiation to the life of the senses and the fulfillment of an instinct by which life itself will be prolonged and immortalized. This act is the only real conquest of a man by which he becomes an ecstatic individual and joins himself with the race of men.

When the sensations of Julien, of Fabrice, of Octave and of Lamiel (in *Lamiel*, Stendhal transposed the sex of his hero into that of a girl) are described in the present, during the course of the novel's action, the novelist is dramatizing his memories. He brought to the analysis of those sensations the greater knowledge, the greater lucidity that the years brought to him. There is no exception to the youthfulness of his heroes. Gide and Mauriac also created many youthful heroes in their novels, but they did not limit them-

selves, as Stendhal did, to a hero in his twenties. The last
chapters of *La Chartreuse de Parme* show us Fabrice del
Dongo after he has passed his youthfulness, but those
chapters are an epilogue to the real novel, which is, as in
every other book, the story of a youthful hero establishing
his first relationship with the world.

Stendhal's hero remains virginal even after he has ac-
complished his first exploits of seducer. His outlook is
virginal. He is always looking at the world for the first
time and wondering about it. His emotions have the delicacy
of a virginal spirit, and he suffers from each disappointment,
from each jolt, as if he were being harmed for the first time.
The novels are an autobiography in retrospect. Even if each
of the heroes appears in a different world and becomes a
member of a different community, the desires of all of them,
their sensitivity, their needs are identical. Stendhal relived
in them his own emotional life, and only partly disguised
the gestures and costumes. His heroes are what he might
have become. They are what he became in his imagination,
in his fantasy-making world.

As meticulous observer of himself, Stendhal has only two
or three rivals in French literature: Montaigne, Gide and
Proust, in particular. This self-observation, carried on from
book to book, dwarfs somewhat his observation of the exterior world, of Verrières or Milan, if one compares Stendhal's art to that of Proust. When Sainte-Beuve accused Stendhal of lacking inventiveness (*homme dénué d'invention*),
he undoubtedly had in mind this recurrence of a similar
hero in each novel. But the critic failed to acknowledge the
novelist's analysis of this hero, an analysis that moves in all
directions and in all degrees of depth. The inventiveness of
Stendhal is in the many varied possible lives his hero can
lead. The heroes are the same youth, but each one is dif-

ferent from the others in the episodes that are often tests of character, in the variety of actions, some of which are based on actual experiences in Stendhal's life and some of which seem to be invented or suggested by known experiences.

Stendhal's inventiveness is his capacity to renew himself, to invent himself, to see himself in a series of circumstances at times similar and at other times dissimilar to circumstances in his own life, to which this endlessly mobile self reacts. A scandal story related in a newspaper or a historical chronicle, found almost by chance, will present sufficient background for *Le Rouge et le Noir* and for *La Chartreuse de Parme*. These settings and these starting points in reality were all that Stendhal needed to convert autobiography into a fictional biography. Essentially he wrote imaginary biographies. The sentimental experiences he had lived through nourished his storyteller's mind. When he turned to history for help, it was never to an official history written by government functionaries or by historians, but to that secret kind of history found in memoirs and letters and journals, in unofficial chronicles that dealt more with the passions of the heart than with reports and treaty agreements.

Sources for each of the major characters of Stendhal have been discovered in documents of one kind or another. It seems largely to have been chance that put these documents into his hands. The books were written by means of a constant correlation between the biographical sources and Stendhal's imagination that dilated on his own autobiography. His books, inspired by dramatic and often melodramatic chronicles, represented his hope of living. They were his hope of living in his mind and in his imagination.

This was his métier, his practice and his method of writing, but it was at the same time far more than that. It was

Henri Beyle's bond with his past. Or rather, it became the means by which Henri Beyle preserved and enshrined his youth. In his books, his youth became his truest reality. No matter how he varies the circumstances of his stories and their historical backgrounds, he does not vary the imaginative life he had led. Stendhal's art is exemplary in this regard.

He himself was so struck by what his books represented, by his strange compulsion to write them, by the need of his nature they satisfied, by the pleasure and the therapeutic cure they provided, that he had to invent a word with which to name this mystery. He used his own name, not his pseudonym, but his family name, by which he was known as a youth. *Le beylisme.* It is the name given by Stendhal to his method. But this method is two things at once: It designates a method in the sense of style and composition, Stendhal's own very recognizable way of writing fiction; and it designates also what was indispensable to that method of writing: a search for happiness. These two words "search" and "happiness" recapitulate Stendhal's life and art. (Later, Marcel Proust will use the same word, *la recherche*, in the title of his novel, and he will refer to Stendhal's phrase in which beauty is defined as "the promise of happiness.")

II

In Search of a Philosophy:

le beylisme

STENDHAL'S OPEN CONFESSION of *le beylisme* is not only a clue to his own art but a major phase in our understanding of the aesthetics of the novel. He always maintained the attitude of a disciple toward those *philosophes* of the eighteenth century and the *idéologues* who wrote during the first years of the nineteenth century. He read them at an early age and continued to read them throughout his life: Helvétius and Condillac, as representatives of eighteenth-century thought, and Destutt de Tracy, one of whose books he claimed to know by heart. Their doctrines, as understood and assimilated by Stendhal, are indispensable to our understanding today of *le beylisme*. What are these doctrines that were revelations for Stendhal?

They center about the belief that all the knowledge of man originates in sensations or in what might be called sense perceptions. In English, this school of thought is usually referred to as sensationalism or sensualism. It is close to empiricism, which is traditionally defined as the pursuit of knowledge by observation and experiment. An out-and-out empiricist attributes the origin of all knowledge to experience. A typical sensualist—Helvétius or Stendhal after him—will tend to explain the problems of the heart and the emotions by the experimental method. Stendhal went as far as to claim that an exact knowledge of facts in a given love affair could lead to happiness. He looked upon the art of the novel as merely one aspect of science. The logical study of phenomena concerned with the emotions accounts for a large part of Stendhal's writings.

Le beylisme is largely preoccupied with method. Emotional states and moral or immoral acts are merely natural phenomena and can be studied in the same way that other natural phenomena are studied. An empiricist searches for truth in a specific way, and a sensualist searches for happiness in a comparable way. Stendhal certainly believed that very few have the will power and the determination to be sensualists. The world calls for conformity to its customs and habits. Stendhal wrote for "the happy few" who are not bound by convention, who do not find their happiness in subservience. The disciple of *le beylisme* follows the lead of his senses and his instincts. He is seen, in the novels of Stendhal, in society, as a member of a social group or on the margin of a social group. But he does not bend to the rules that this society tries to impose upon him. Each hero of Stendhal is presented as being opposed to the social world he lives in and serves.

In stressing traits of singularity in each hero, Stendhal separates him from the social group. The members of the Faubourg Saint-Germain will end by being suspicious of Octave de Malivert in *Armance,* and Julien Sorel from the beginning of *Le Rouge et le Noir* is despised by his father and his brothers. The Stendhalian hero casts doubt over every habit and every characteristic of society. Even the most fervent signs of friendship have elements of selfishness that Stendhal's protagonists will point out, not necessarily as serious moral blemishes, but as phenomena that have to be recognized and acknowledged. Distrust, at least to a mild degree, is a constant attitude of Julien and Octave, of Fabrice and Lucien. The innumerable minute discoveries that are made by the hero, because of this distrust, form the body of facts by which an individual is known, by which one man becomes a distinct reality. This slow accumulation of facts is the method by which an individual is known and the world around him is known.

In Stendhal's system, sentiments and morality can play no part in the accumulation of these facts. They would be obstacles in the search, they would defeat the objectivity of the search. Sentiment and morality would lead to fallacy and dishonesty. They would tend to alter the facts. If there were any trace of dishonesty, the goal of the search—happiness— would be obscured and lost sight of. Stendhal knew that the society of which he was a part (and he would apply this to societies before and after his) was so controlled by forces of authority, by the police, by the army, by public opinion, that it was impossible for a man to escape being a hypocrite. Everything forced him to conceal his real thoughts, to cover up the differences between him and other men. Hypocrisy was a way of life in Stendhal's world, and that is why he emphasized in his stories, and often in a melodramatic way, the use of secret papers, concealed orders, spies, pseudonyms, passwords. A world of suspicion is a world of disguises. The secrecy and gadgetry of James Bond's world are not unlike Stendhal's.

If happiness is the goal of man, in order to reach it in
such a complex world as the Empire—which witnessed the
fall of Napoleon, the Restoration of the Bourbons and the
Revolution of 1830—a man had to calculate his moves,
estimate his chances, practice flattery, quite literally construct his happiness on his knowledge of the ways of man
and his skill at exploiting those ways. In many of his letters
to Pauline, Beyle acknowledged the change he underwent
when he began to understand reasons for some of his defeats
in life and the ruses he would have to practice and cultivate.

Not only did Henri Beyle come to recognize evil in the
world, but he undertook the study of its causes. Throughout
this program of *beylisme,* despite the seemingly scientific
coldness of the method, despite the clearheaded determined
Machiavellism that was part of it, Beyle never lost any of
his acute sensitivity to reproof and criticism, but he an-
guished over every minor and every major defeat. The
harshness of the program never diminished the delicacy of
his feelings and the suffering he felt from every trace of the
world's hostility.

With the example of Helvétius before him, and even of
the seventeenth-century moralist La Rochefoucauld, Beyle
never varied from his conviction that egoism, man's self-
interest, is the sole motivation of all his actions. Every one
of our actions may be useful in terms of the happiness we
are trying to reach. This happiness is not an abstract idea
or an impossibility. It can be reached by the judicious use
of our reason, and by our will power. But it is indispensable
to employ the strategy of warfare, to plan our attacks, to
use devices, tricks and ruses. Human nature is such, and
society is such, that religion and moral injunctions have to
be put aside. There is nothing mystical about happiness, in
Beyle's conception. It is comparable to a mathematical

demonstration. The world is the enemy, and it has to be fought with the full knowledge that it is the enemy.

So, not from Voltaire, whom he did not like, but from the encyclopedists, especially from Helvétius, Beyle derived his "method," which made out of man's actions a fully conscious means of materialistic and sensuous enjoyment of life. Beyle's originality was the new goal he gave to this method. His word "happiness" (*bonheur*) does not correspond to the goal of an Helvétius or a Condillac. Whereas the encyclopedists were intent upon discovering the mechanics of pleasure, Beyle was intent upon discovering the mechanics of happiness.

The ultimate meaning of happiness for Beyle went far beyond the materialistic and sensual goal of pleasure for Helvétius. Whereas the point of departure in Beyle's search was materialistic and frankly objective—in keeping with eighteenth-century philosophy—the final goal, the happiness of the soul, the discovery of the deepest energies of the soul, was a spiritual acquisition very much in keeping with the philosophy of Jean-Jacques Rousseau and the aspirations of the romantics. In more ways than one, Beyle's method for reaching happiness contradicts the avowed goal of happiness. Is it contradiction or reconciliation? Can the functioning of man's intelligence—in his determination to overcome all threats of the world, all machinations that would impede his bodily and his social pleasures—lead to that exaltation of the heart where all worldly ambitions are surpassed? Beyle's nature was far less that of a philosopher than that of an artist. He reduced the antinomy between method and goal, between eighteenth-century philosophy and romantic idealism, by creating in hero after hero a series of strategic actions destined to encourage and promote the most delirious of passions. Each one of these heroes, by the practice of his intelligence and by the needs of his sensibility, joins the politics of action with the ecstasy of sentimental feeling. The originality of Stendhal's art is precisely in this merger.

After his first brief but strong infatuation with Italian society and the cultural life of Milan, between 1800 and 1801, Beyle's desire to be a writer grew more and more imperious. He found an easy pretext (the peace of Amiens) to resign from the army and settled down in Paris, in a small rented room, where he began a period of study, as preparation for making himself a writer of comedies in the tradition of Molière and Shakespeare. He believed he could learn about man's psychological life by studying the treatises of Destutt de Tracy and the minor philosophers of the eighteenth century, Helvétius and Cabanis, in particular. The initial reason for this study was to develop in himself the power to create in his plays characters that would possess the credibility and universality of Molière's. The study would enable him better to understand other human beings as well as to understand himself.

Henri Beyle set out, then, to understand the human system, to understand how an individual and how society function. The first lesson he learned from Tracy and Helvétius and Cabanis was to discover that principles should be the guide for human behavior rather than sensations and that the nurturing of a critical spirit would be more efficacious than a dependence on spontaneous reactions and natural behavior. As he worked on projects for plays, he outlined at the same time ways of winning the attention of women, ways of behaving in a salon, ways of knowing how to react to unpredictable social situations.

This was the time in Beyle's life when, by means of correspondence, he educated his sister Pauline in social comportment and discipline. At the same time he was teaching himself. His letters were compositions on philosophy and psychology, lessons derived from Condillac and Corneille. He was simultaneously autodidact and teacher. As he grew in knowledge and pedantic habits, he ironically achieved less and less in his specific goals: the writing of good comedies and the attainment to amorous and social conquests. Strict adherence to a method did not seem to assure young Beyle of scriptorial success and success with women. In his notebooks he wrote out the clear engineering-like plans for his strategy. But the notebooks contain also the record of his failures. The willfully imposed method seemed to kill the naturalness of the man's behavior and the easy-flowing spontaneity of his writing. Between 1802 and 1806 he forced himself to study an eighteenth-century scientifically conceived method designed to enable a man to reach happiness.

Napoleon's fall in 1814 caused the collapse of Beyle's political career. He was about to be appointed to an important *préfecture* at that time. So he left Paris for Milan, where he lived thanks to a veteran's pension, and had considerable time for the arts and the theater, for social life and for writing.

As mentioned earlier, he met Métilde Dembowska in Milan. More than any other woman she taught him the meaning of despair and frustration. But this experience revived in him the conviction that a man's happiness is to be found in his aspiration for love rather than in a dry philosophical system that is planned in advance and one that leaves nothing open and free for the development of a man's instincts.

When he returned to Paris in 1821, he had made marked progress in his social success, in his role of conversationalist and writer, in the skill with which he could flatter and please beautiful women. In the 1820s Beyle was a very different man from the young autodidact who stayed in his own room most of the time during the first years of the century. *De l'Amour* was the analysis of his sentiments not only about love but about himself in 1821 and 1822. He had learned to take pleasure from meetings with friends, on Tuesday evenings, for example, at the house of Mme. Ancelot, on Sunday evenings, at the home of M. de Tracy. It was now easy for him to adapt to any social group. To some extent at least, he now resembled the type of polished gentleman he was to portray in M. Leuwen (*Lucien Leuwen*) and Count Mosca (*La Chartreuse de Parme*). During the decade of the twenties his Paris social life expanded considerably, and he felt increasingly at ease in the many social groups he frequented. He grew almost to like Paris, but he never completely forgave Paris society for its lack of naturalness, for its unwillingness to express its feelings directly. Italy, again, after 1830 and the publication of *Le Rouge et le Noir*, became the scene where Stendhal continued his search for happiness and for a philosophy that would permit this happiness to be reached.

Stendhal never attained to the status of a philosopher, but he was throughout his life a theorist, in an almost naïve way. He remained a serious student of philosophy, hopeful that if he studied hard enough, analyzed enough dry treatises on human conduct and outlined their contents, he would be able to see, in a meaningful chart, the variety of human temperaments. Before becoming a great novelist in 1830, Stendhal had been a student for thirty years, in a decidedly pedantic way, of human passions. He had been a student of those French philosophers who were the first psychologists to look upon psychology as a science, and whose works are today quite forgotten.

Literary creation is indeed a mysterious alchemy, when one considers that such creatures as Julien Sorel and Gina Sanseverina are the products of a man's mind that owe at least something to the writings of Cabanis, Condillac, Helvétius and Tracy. In classifying, in such a methodical way, the sentiments of man for his sister Pauline, Henri Beyle was trying to find equations that would explain all the storms of love and all the dramas of passion. He was pretentious only in the sense that all naïve students of psychology are pretentious in their earnest conviction that formulas can be found that will explain coldly and scientifically the behavior of man and teach him how to live at greater peace with himself and the world.

During the first years of the Empire, Beyle studied such works as *La Logique* of Tracy, which proposed a method of positivistic research, *Le Traité des sensations* of Condillac, and especially two works of Helvétius, *L'Esprit* and *L'Homme*, which were based on the principle that all of man's ideas come from his senses. These were the sensualist philosophers who led Stendhal to believe that man can be refashioned as if he were a machine. In *L'Idéologie* of Tracy, he studied the ways in which the faculties of man can be analyzed, the precise way sentiments can be understood in the light of circumstances affecting temperaments. The physician Cabanis emphasized the way in which a man is dependent upon his physical environment and explained by it.

Such readings as these, annotated by Beyle as if they were the program of a university course, clearly indicate that his intellectual leanings were not those of the romantics, of Mme. de Staël and Chateaubriand, but were similar to the interests of the eighteenth-century *philosophes*. Chronologically he preceded the romantic school and was educated during the Revolution in one of the Ecoles Centrales, founded by the Revolution. This type of education, which was to be of a short duration, was based on logical reasoning and on scientific observation.

Stendhal was the only French writer of note to receive such an education, and to follow it up with extensive readings from the so-called *idéologues*. His genius cannot be explained by his study of the *idéologues*, but they do account for the originality of his intellectual position that sets him apart from the French romantic writers. The rigors of scientific analysis, which attracted him, and the appeal of logic are not totally absent from the mental constitution of Fabrice del Dongo and Octave and Julien Sorel.

The ideology of the eighteenth century that Beyle studied was the natural method of French classicism, clearly visible in Descartes and Malebranche. It is the method of mathematics, by which very simple, very general notions are isolated and circumscribed. When these notions are combined and compared, the consequences are reached by pure reasoning. In their studies of sensations and primitive instincts, such *idéologues* as Condillac, Condorcet, Cabanis and Tracy follow similar methods of research. They tend to remain on the surface of an experiment and never move deeply within it for details and characteristic examples.

La Logique of Condillac and *L'Idéologie* of Destutt de Tracy do not provide examples and specimens one might expect for such research. They offer no examples of personal observations, but remain in the rarefied atmosphere of pure generalities, of what they liked to call "pure ideas." Condillac insisted that psychological research can be carried out as if it were mathematics, that the elements of man's thinking are analogous to arithmetical formulas. The philosopher Siéyès claimed that politics is a science that can be mastered in the way that Descartes mastered analytical geometry. The paucity of examples and the unwillingness to rely on facts, which characterize the writings of the *philosophes*, are clear in Destutt de Tracy's complaint about Montesquieu, when he said that Montesquieu as historian remained too close to history! It would be more suitable for an historian, according to Tracy, to construct an ideal society than to describe society as it is. Rousseau needed only a contract by means of which he founded a political association. From such meagerness, he constructed the constitution, the government and the laws of a just society.

Henri Beyle felt kinship with the *idéologues*. He was a friend of Destutt de Tracy whom he looked upon as a master of analysis, capable of teaching him the science of the soul. When Stendhal observed one given character, he believed he was studying man. Knowledge concerning one individual would lead him to knowledge concerning the human species. This background in reading accounts to some degree for the impression that *Le Rouge et le Noir* gives of being a psychology in action. An entire theory of human passions could be extracted from it because of the large number of inconspicuous little facts to which people (readers) ordinarily do not pay attention.

Stendhal's art, which he will develop especially in *Le Rouge et le Noir* and *La Chartreuse de Parme*, is the opposite of Racine's art in which characters analyze directly their emotions by means of long speeches. A psychoanalyst would probably claim that such elaborate self-analysis at moments of crisis in a tragedy detracts from the truthfulness of the statements. Stendhal's novels come closer to revealing the truth concerning emotion by showing the variety of a man's sentiments, the swiftness with which they come and go, their unpredictable variations and changes, the total lack of oratorical rhetoric in the manner by which they are communicated to the reader. In his oratory and dramatic movements, Racine is primarily a poet. In his observation of actions and gestures, Stendhal is primarily a psychologist.

Of all the subjects open to him for choice as a novelist, Stendhal will elect that subject which is closest to the concern of the *idéologues*, the life of the soul. By such a phrase is meant the characteristics of a personality, the sentiments of the personality and the vicissitudes of the passion that affect the personality. Stendhal will be as capable of describing a landscape as Rousseau was in *La Nouvelle Héloïse*, as capable of describing the clothes and the house of his characters as Balzac was and as capable of constructing a plot as Prévost was. But all of that interests him much less than the challenge of following the thoughts and the emotions going on inside of his characters. He will avoid telling the dramatic events of his stories in a dramatic way, in order better to follow the story of the heart, the somewhat concealed drama of the heart.

The story of Julien Sorel ends with his execution, but Stendhal has no interest in exploiting such a situation, such a spectacle. We do not see the gallows and the blood. The scene is described by avoiding the melodramatic. The rich full sunlight of the day is described, and the freshness of the air that Julien breathes, and the courage he feels, and the memory he has of a comparable moment in the woods of Vergy when he had looked up at the sky. In terms of the plot, Julien's execution is the principal scene in *Le Rouge et le Noir*, and no other scene would lend itself so easily to a spectacular melodramatic treatment.

Stendhal limits himself to recording the sentiments of an ambitious boy and describing the customs of the social groups in which he lives. That is all. In his study of the *idéologues* and in his search for a guiding philosophy, Stendhal came to believe that a thought, a passion, an impulse of the soul were more significant than the clothes his hero wore, the house in which he lived and the adventures he had. The adventure going on in the mind of Julien Sorel touches all the rest, but it is that adventure that concerns Stendhal the novelist. Facts, ideas and sentiments are matters that a novelist can attempt to analyze in words and that a painter cannot depict in forms and colors. The details of a house or a landscape have some importance for Stendhal only if they bear a relationship with the inner psyche and the moral life of his character.

In his determination to analyze those minute and often inconspicuous mental processes that form and explain a personality, he elected a superior type of character. But not heroic in the traditional sense. Julien, Octave and Fabrice are all exceptional young men—original, unique and very real characters—totally different from the ordinary run-of-the-mill character. They are not great men, however. They are not heroes as a Corneille would understand a hero. They are memorable, but they are not men who would be imitated by their youthful readers.

Of all of Stendhal's characters, Julien Sorel is presented with the greatest detail and is the most fully known by the reader. Yet, he is the strangest of the characters, and, in that sense, is the most unknown. All extremes of impulse and nature meet in him and in dizzying sequences: timidity and boldness at the beginning of the novel, and from that point on goodness of heart and selfishness, naïveté in behavior and

reflection at times being offset by an extraordinary shrewdness in calculating the effects of planned behavior. He is
both child and diplomat.

In his depiction of Julien Sorel, how does Stendhal account for the contradictions in the boy's actions and in his
feelings? Are these contradictions what Stendhal means by
naturalness of behavior? Stendhal would argue that the
actions and the sentiments of Julien are true because they
follow the logic of the heart. The mainspring of his behavior is his pride, an excessive and passionate pride that is
constantly being hurt in his relationships with everyone. He
is also endowed with a lively imagination that generates a
multitude of ideas at every event, at every slight occurrence,
and that allows him to be absorbed in these ideas.

Such is Julien's pattern of behavior and reaction that
keeps him uninterruptedly concentrated on himself, indulging in a self-examination in order to construct an ideal
picture of himself, a model with whom he contrasts his real
self in order to measure how close he is coming to matching
the model. Conformity with the model is his duty. He often
analyzes what he considers weaknesses in his character. He
accuses himself of indulging in emotional outbursts. The
disparity between the model he wishes to emulate and the
real Julien is the explanation, the well-nigh scientific explanation of Julien's sentiments and actions.

The need in Julien to approach the example of the second lieutenant who became emperor explains the boy's
disgust over his shortcomings and his hopes for himself. At
home with his father and brothers, his dominant need that
fashioned his ideas was that of finding some way to escape
from the humiliation and the dependency that the poverty
of his family and their hostile feelings toward him created.
To escape from the vulgarity of his home is Julien's first

stratagem. The picture he has of his family is his first picture of society. As a child and young boy, his war with his
family will be continued in his war with society, with the
bourgeois elements of M. de Rênal's family in Verrières, with
the aristocratic elements of the Marquis de la Mole's family
in Paris. Julien never ceased being the enemy of whatever
social group he lived with. Even if his basic instincts were
tender and loving, he had trained himself in his home to
be egotistical and to exploit those human beings he encountered in his life. Julien Sorel was a fundamentally good
man, but he learned early in life to destroy whatever stood
in his way to happiness.

As if he were a scientist checking the facts of an experiment in a laboratory, Julien weighed and examined minute
details that had come to his attention as a young boy and
reached the verifiable conclusions that his future lay in the
priesthood. His strategy began with his courting and flatter-
ing a priest and learning Latin from an old army surgeon.
These seemingly hypocritical actions were the only way open
to him. Little wonder that every day a storm waged in
Julien's heart because of the vastness of his dream and the
petty advances or the failures he made daily in carrying out
his plans and his attacks. As he grew more and more skilled
in his social behavior, his distrust of all of mankind grew
proportionately. He feared in himself traits of awkwardness
and ridiculousness only when his goal became magnified in
his mind and assumed proportions far beyond any possible
achievement.

When he felt himself loved by his friend Fouqué and by
the parish priest Chélan and by Abbé Pirard, he was tortured
by fear that he might misbehave with regard to them. Nothing
is easy for this egotist who has the capacity and feelings of
outgoing affection. In obeying all the plottings and plans of

his pride, he does not eradicate the causes for his emotional upheavals. A detailed study of Julien's character would show how totally different he is from the characters of Corneille and Racine, of Mme. de Lafayette and La Bruyère. He is complex and multiple. He is contradictory and original as men are who live a day-to-day life. Julien and all of the leading characters of Stendhal are presented as living from day to day, with all the monotonous daily occurrences that compose a life, and at the same time they are superior to all those in whose company they live. Their superiority is in their taste, in their thoughts, in their sentiments, and often in their actions. Their strength of conviction is their moral beauty. Whereas Corneille's heroes—a Rodrigue, a Horace, a Polyeucte—appear as models for a form of moral behavior, Stendhal's heroes never appear as models to be imitated but as young men whose lives present to the reader a multiplicity of moral and psychological questions he would like to understand and that he follows in the novels with unabated interest.

As a reader of the *idéologues,* Stendhal was made aware of the power of words, of the power that words have to suggest and to instigate ideas in the mind of a character. Whenever a moment of passion is reached in any of Stendhal's characters, the forcefulness of words, as they flash through the character's mind, conduct and control the thoughts about the passion and the very forcefulness of the passion. When Mme. de Rênal first feels love for Julien, she enjoys the thoughts of her new happiness as she remembers the passionate kisses with which Julien covered her hand. Then suddenly the word "adultery" comes to her mind, and the power of this word transforms her imagination, transforms the images of happiness she has allowed to grow in her mind. Her feelings at that moment are quite literally governed by the shocking forcefulness of a single word. Words contain the ideas that account for our moral life and our sensual life. The almost holy image that Mme. de Rênal has of Julien's love for her is suddenly tarnished by the word *adultère* and by the idea it represents to her.

This passage in *Le Rouge et le Noir,* among countless others throughout Stendhal's fictional writings, indicates that the struggle over passion takes place in the realm of ideas. Mme. de Rênal's love for Julien is projected by means of two conflicting ideas that torment her: the desire for Julien and the thought that this desire is immoral. A character in love is not portrayed by Stendhal as always being in love. The love a character feels for another person is constantly being degraded by thoughts that imperil it. Julien— endowed with a very active imagination, and this is a characteristic of Stendhal's characters—is constantly fluctuating because of the multiplicity of sensations that affect him and that derange the ordered logic of his plans. The sensations of the moment are often stronger than the abstract ideas he has defined for himself and combined into a system of strategy.

A Stendhal character is a man in possession of a certain number of ideas that are calculated to guide his life. Stendhal's art of a novelist is in the way the character uses these ideas, how he combines them in terms of his actions, and how he modifies them in terms of the unexpected happenings in his life that affect his senses and his sentiments. The character never presents his ideas blatantly as if they were comparable to some fixed value that could never be altered. In other words, Stendhal presents his characters in action, without providing a commentary. Facts, movements, gestures speak for themselves.

The novelist is not the actor for Stendhal, who by his histrionics forces the reader to believe such and such a thing about a given character. The actor in the book is the character himself. Stendhal's voice is silenced. The novelist's own personality never transcends that of Julien or Fabrice, of Mathilde or La Sanseverina. The ensemble of the book is sustained by logic and not by emotions. It is an art of argument and proof. In the course of the narration, the only tone that would be Stendhal's and not the tone of his characters is a sympathetic understanding that is often slightly ironical. In his feelings for mankind and for his characters Stendhal does reveal an almost imperceptible tender irony. At no point is this attitude cutting or devastating.

In the salon scenes of the novels, there are countless portraits of secondary characters, briefly sketched but very clear. These scenes are the reporting of a very keen observer of human traits and idiosyncrasies, of a man who writes freshly and directly his impressions of a character he sees, and who never judges his impressions with any degree of prejudice. Stendhal is never the moralist. He has nothing about him of the professional expert. He suppresses in his writing those traits that would mark him as the writer concerned with careful phrasing and rhetorical effects and psychological evaluations. The naturalness of Stendhal's style is in keeping with the freshness of his observations. Stendhal writes about a moral world, but not as a moralist and not as a rhetorician.

The incisiveness of his writing comes from his perceptions that are cast in a totally simple form. If there is to be any value judgment about his characters, that is left up to the reader. Julien Sorel's reactions to M. de Rênal's home in Verrières, to the seminary in Besançon and to the *hôtel* of M. de la Mole in Paris come to him so fast and in such abundance that there is literally no time to draw up co-

herent judgments. Dialogues and narrations of small events
provide the substance of the novels. For a superior mind like
Stendhal's, that is enough communication to make to the
"happy few."

The methodical observation within this philosophy, which
is called *beylisme,* is a creative process because it is so markedly suggestive and enriching. The soul of a character is con-
tained within any one of his gestures, any one of his traits.
It is in a single action, whether the action be fortuitous or
adventurous or planned. The philosophy of *beylisme* is expressed in the form of a drama whenever a character, such
as Julien, is in conflict with his society. Stendhal's personal
drama is recast in all of his heroes' conflicts. The hero is
attracted by the glittering promises that the world seems to
make to him. These promises are always made to appear easy
to realize. But then gradually as the hero faces the world and
engages in the first skirmishes, he receives the first wounds.
Most of these attacks on him seem minute and inconsequential, but with their accumulation, his attitude toward
the world changes. A loathing for the world he has set out
to conquer grows in him, although his appetite for happiness never diminishes.

The meaning of *beylisme* has deepened and become increasingly clear with the passing of four generations since
Stendhal's death in 1842. The late romantics—Balzac in
particular—the generation of Taine and the subsequent
generation represented by Paul Bourget have described
Stendhal as the analyst, as the egotist and as the champion
of energy. But today with the new critics, men like Georges
Poulet and Jean Starobinski, Stendhal's doctrine seems pre-
dominantly concerned with the concept of happiness. That
energy once spoken of as action is now seen to be the forcefulness of the heart.

The elaborate reading program and the studies that Stendhal carried out in the early years of the century in Paris are comparable to his heroes' preparation for their conquest of the world in the early part of the stories. He wanted first to develop, for his talent of a writer, a solid philosophical basis. Then he drew up plans consciously and methodically, with that kind of determination he puts into the characters of Julien and Fabrice. And yet Stendhal never believed, even in the early years of his studies, that he would make any startling discoveries of a psychological or philosophical nature. He simply believed that philosophical studies were indispensable for his future career. A philosophical bent would be for him an invaluable support for his talent of a dramatist and novelist. He repeated this conviction several times in his personal writing of 1804–1805 (*Pensées, Journal*). He even planned the writing of an elaborate philosophical discourse (*Filosofia nova*) destined to help him in the writing of future works.

Stendhal's attitude toward the *philosophes* was usually admiring, but on occasion he was critical as in his *Pensées* where he indicated differences of opinion. His early enthusiasm for Helvétius changed when he began to feel that the philosopher judged men as being more reasonable than they are. To Stendhal, men appeared more dominated by passion than by reason. Passion was for Stendhal the clue to friendship and love. In letters to Pauline, in 1804, Stendhal expressed doubt over the originality of ideas in Helvétius, and concluded that he was not the great philosopher, the *maître* that he had once believed him to be.

At this point in his studies, Stendhal was beginning to ascribe more and more importance to the function of a man's sensibility, and hence less importance to the role of his reason. In his notes for his *philosophie nouvelle* he wrote that he had begun to study the distinction between *heart* and *understanding* (*coeur* and *tête*). This distinction was to be one of the bases of his philosophy. In this investigation Stendhal followed quite closely the argument of Lancelin's *Introduction à l'analyse des sciences,* which he had been reading at least since 1803. But interest in Lancelin does not seem to have lasted beyond 1804.

At the end of 1804 Stendhal's discovery of Destutt de Tracy was to have a marked influence on the development of his ideas. He had already recommended to his sister the reading of Tracy's *Idéologie.* On the last day of the year he bought a copy of the work and during the next few days in January 1805 commented in his *Journal* on the satisfaction he derived from the reading. In a letter to Pauline, he outlined the contents of the first two chapters of the *Idéologie* and added explanations of his own. He found in Tracy an analysis of the functioning of the mind, the mechanics of the intellectual faculties, a theory on the identifying of thinking and feeling (*penser* and *sentir*), the theory that judging means simply the understanding of relationships between ideas; the definitions of the four elementary faculties: sensibility, memory, judgment and will; the theory that such judgments are the basis of our knowledge.

Stendhal was immediately won over to Tracy and he was to consider himself a disciple of Tracy for the rest of his life. The *Idéologie* was the clearest explanation of human nature that he ever found in philosophical works. In his *Journal* entry of January 7, he asked himself the question, "What constitutes a great character?" (*Qu'est-ce qu'un grand caractère?*). And he pointed out that the very idea of the question was the result of his reading of the *Idéologie* of Tracy. From his reading of Tracy and Maine de Biran (*Influence de l'habitude sur la faculté de penser*), Stendhal extracted what he needed for the clarification of his own ideas as he explored the major problems related to ideology and to physiology.

The motivations in Stendhal for such extensive study and research were many. In part, the study aimed at the acquisition of a culture and knowledge, at training in method that might help him to write comedies that would continue for his day the tradition of Molière. In part, it would help him to observe more keenly and to understand the actions and the motivations behind the actions. But there were also deeply personal reasons. Such a study might well be a compensation for his shortcomings. It might help cover up his lack of skill in conversation, his total lack of close friends in whom he might confide. It might help him reach a greater truth about himself.

Stendhal's solitude and his temperament with its tendency toward melancholy account to some degree for his long study, which was, among other things, a therapeutic exercise for him. He feared mediocrity. He doubted his intellectual and social capacities. With such besetting doubts about himself, his place is close to that of the most famous self-doubters in French literature: Montaigne and Gide. He needed to examine himself, and his writing was the practice of self-discipline, self-development and self-clarification. In his personal writings, *Vie de Henry Brulard* and his *Journal,* as well as in his fiction, Stendhal and his heroes are concerned with ways of changing themselves, altering their habits, revising their views, as Montaigne does in the *Essais* and as Gide does in such a book as *Si le grain ne meurt.* The problem of moral behavior is uppermost in all three French writers. They are all adverse to the conventions of behavior.

The world created by Stendhal in all of his writings is a moral world, as moral as that created by the *essais* of Michel de Montaigne and the *récits* of André Gide. But it is not easy to define the precise kind of morality that prevails in it. He is not as coherent a moralist as either Montaigne or Gide. Is his search for happiness merely a form of epicureanism or even a dilettantism? Is his determination to reach a high degree of lucidity merely the application of a Voltairian principle? Is his cult of energy, of *espagnolisme,* a form of mysticism, or a form of heroism that later in Europe will be associated with Nietzsche?

The ways in which Stendhal trained himself to enjoy the arts, the beauty of painting and of music, revealed an epicurean side of his nature. His dreams of an existence with enough income to assure himself of the usual comforts and more: a carriage, a box at the opera, a house where he could adequately receive his friends were the dreams of an epicurean, of a mind that considered itself superior and privileged and that yearned to find the means whereby he could lead a certain kind of life.

But Stendhal's heroes were not so socially and aesthetically limited in their aims. Julien committed a crime in the name of passion. Lucien was motivated by a passionate love. Fabrice had in him a boldness and a fervor of spirit that were not the traits of gentlemen in society. Stendhal was motivated not only by epicureanism but also, in the portrayal of his leading characters, by an exalted form of heroism, by a *virtù* that recalled the Renaissance, by a willingness to risk everything, life and fortune, if the risk were worthy of a hero.

The contradictions between the epicureanism of Stendhal's nature and the bold heroism of his fictional heroes are fused and harmonized in *le beylisme,* which is the summation of his philosophy. Long before it was defined as such, *le beÿlisme,* even in its most tentative form, separated Henri Beyle from the early romantics, from Chateaubriand and Lamartine and also from the later more rebellious youthful spirits of Les Jeune-France. The romantics themselves were equally disdainful of Stendhal and treated him condescendingly as a writer. They acknowledged him as a man of talent, but not more than that. By the time of Stendhal's death only one article of any importance on his work had appeared, Balzac's article on *La Chartreuse de Parme.* Outside of France Goethe had paid attention to Stendhal and had expressed his admiration for *Le Rouge et le Noir.*

The subtlety of the term *beylisme,* which is largely philosophical, lies in its implications of ardent sentiments on the one hand and precise facts prepared in an orderly logical manner on the other hand. *Beylisme* is a fusion or a confusion of the spiritual and the material. Its development in the thought and the writing of Stendhal is one aspect at least in the more general development of the positivistic spirit in the nineteenth century and in the critical spirit of the twentieth century.

Stendhal's brief curt analysis of ideas, the swift precision in his writing by which he describes the influence of an environment or a character, the clipped way in which a fact is inserted in a passage are all parts of Stendhal's literary style, as well as parts of his method of accumulating facts that tend toward a positivistic critical approach that is developed later in the century with Taine and the realists. Stendhal was not inclined to correct and rewrite. His sentences are often rhythmically monotonous and his adjectives repetitious. Even a style characterized by bareness and simplicity has to be polished and perfected.

An absence of any recognizable literary style is Stendhal's

style, and this seems to be in keeping with the scientific or documentary part of his writing. He wants neither artfulness nor scientific documentation to dominate. Passages in his *Journal* reveal a fairly constant preoccupation with the study and formulation of a philosophy, which is accompanied by a need to perfect his style, to develop the precision, clarity and accuracy of his sentences. When he acknowledges his lack of skill in expressing the profoundest shadings of sentiments and meanings, simply because he cannot find adequate terms, he reminds us of the writer's scruples and torments that we have come to associate mainly with Flaubert . . . *les nuances fines, le profond, le meilleur* . . . When such difficulties arise, Stendhal solves them by having recourse to using those words and phrases that come to his mind first, those verbal utterances that are the primitive expression of the idea. These he trusts as being the more truthful to the idea, even if they are not totally satisfactory. He will sacrifice the refinement of a literary style for a closer adherence to the idea as it first occurs in his mind.

Flaubert denounced such habits visible in Stendhal's writing as negligences of style, but Taine defended Stendhal as being bent, primarily, on giving an idea its clearest possible expression and therefore willingly suppressed any flourish or adornment. As much as any writer, Stendhal suffered from the difficulty of transplanting the substance of his thought into words. But he wrote swiftly, as one inspired, and did not return to his writing to polish it and recast it. He was a writer who reached his style in the first draft. This is probably because he wrote when he was elated and enthusiastic about writing, when he had to write in order to give vent to his emotions and his thoughts.

The bareness of Stendhal's style, quite comparable to Voltaire's, has preserved the freshness and directness of his writing for more than one hundred years. His writing has no particular age, because it has neither the lushness of the romantic style, nor the labored meticulousness of the Parnassian style. The style of writing, so centrally characteristic of the eighteenth century and eminently displayed in Voltaire, was appropriated by Stendhal because he had read so much of it, and when he wrote he submitted it to even greater leanness and alertness. His style seems today more unequal and ageless than the style of Chateaubriand, Flaubert and Proust. It belongs to no literary fashion, or rather it belongs to that style of writing best exemplified in the twentieth century by Gide, where the expression and the thought are married and consubstantial, where the ideas are the style and where the idiosyncratic tendencies of a literary school are nonexistent. . . . All of this is perhaps equivalent to saying that Stendhal is what he is: a psychologist, a story-teller, a philosopher of happiness, without appearing to be so. Henri Beyle became Stendhal effortlessly, unostentatiously.

III

Stendhal as Critic

De l'Amour IS A CURIOUS BOOK that does have a plan, visible especially at the beginning but ultimately obscured by the multiplicity of themes and bits of information and by a general medley of theories and personal memories. Stendhal announces four kinds of love, and then elects one in which he speaks of seven moments. Of these seven moments, he analyzes the fifth and the seventh, the two moments of "crystallization." The confusion of the book seems to come from an overly meticulous announcement of parts that are not studied. The theory of *cristallisation* seems to take precedence over the theory of love.

The book is closely associated with Stendhal's deep love for Métilde Viscontini, who, when the book was first conceived and written, around 1820, was living in Milan, separated from her husband Jean Dembowski. At one moment when Métilde asked Stendhal to stop writing to her, he began the writing of a novel about her that is now referred to as *Le roman de Métilde*. There are traces of this projected novel in *De l'Amour,* where some of the very personal chapters, such as the explanation of the lover's awkwardness, are best understood by Stendhal's relationship with Métilde.

De l'Amour is, first, a defense of love addressed to the beloved, and then it is a critical treatise on love. There are traces in it of Destutt de Tracy's book on love. In a preface to the book, which he wrote much later, in 1842, Stendhal claims the idea began with his jotting down anecdotes about the subject of love on the program of a concert. Evidently many anecdotes and stories he originally planned to include were suppressed. But the leading ideas seem to come from anecdotes. The form of the book—the sequence of the ideas and their illustrations—is constantly being blurred and modified by the details.

Stendhal first studies the emergence of the sentiment of love as explained by his theory of crystallization. Then he analyzes certain aspects of passion that are explained by the inhibitions caused by the presence of the beloved and the purely cerebral or imaginative enjoyment of passion. The lover has to learn how to feel what the beloved feels. This is an art that has to be acquired. Another part of the book studies love in terms of the various temperaments of the lover, and the influence on love of climate, customs and social institutions. This summary of themes indicates a more organized plan than the book actually possesses. It is in reality a collection of thoughts on love, of maxims, some of which are expressed vigorously and eloquently.

The tone of the writing changes from chapter to chapter. The sentences often resemble formulas, and they seem to gravitate around the same idea and to support the general thesis that Stendhal is trying to communicate. The problem of composition in this critical treatise that Stendhal never solves is how to join the fragments out of which the book is composed. He uses an anecdote by announcing it awkwardly, rather than by some way in which it might grow out from the text as an integral part of it.

In this book, which is far more a personal confession than a philosophical treatise, Stendhal studies mainly the form of love he calls *amour-passion,* or that kind of love Héloïse felt for Abélard. The other three forms: *amour-goût, amour-physique, amour-vanité,* receive less attention. These four types are combined with six possible temperaments, of which the first four are the temperaments of man according to seventeenth-century medicine: sanguine, bilious, melancholic, phlegmatic, athletic and nervous. In the genesis and development of love three movements are distinguishable: admiration, hope and crystallization (*admiration, espérance, cristallisation*). The moment of crystallization itself has two distinct periods: a moment of revery when future joys are imagined, and a second moment when the revery presents a picture of perfect happiness.

Love, for Stendhal, is a state of feeling that stimulates the intelligence. Then the intelligence, in its turn, stimulates the heart. *La cristallisation* is the reflective thoughtful part of the process. As soon as a lover thinks of a perfection in the beloved, he sees it in her. "What I call crystallization," writes Stendhal, "is the mental operation that draws everything from the discovery that the beloved has new perfections." Crystallization is the unparalleled joy of youthful love which finds in the beloved perfections that others cannot see. With experience and the passing of time, Stendhal claims that distrust grows in the love experience and diminishes the power of crystallization.

The book is basically pedagogic. Stendhal admires woman as being more sentimental than intelligent, but as being spiritually the equal of man. The text has its place in the development of *le beylisme* because it is a study of the conditions for happiness. In his analysis of *l'amour-passion,* he gives to the emotions in a man that come from dreams of love, a higher value than the emotions he derives from actual physical possession of woman. In writing *De l'Amour,* Stendhal unquestionably wanted to be a clinical scientist, the man carefully charting the entire scheme and importance of love. But he is not that. He remains the artist in his analysis, the lyricist who is paying homage to the experience of love, an almost chivalric homage that often belies the epicureanism of other writings of his. He is the memorialist in *De l'Amour,* the man recording the most memorable experience of the writer, both cruel and exalted memories.

De l'Amour had almost no readers at first. The book has taken a long time to occupy any place at all in Stendhal studies. Even such a theory as *la cristallisation* has taken considerable time to be accepted and known. But a short literary pamphlet, written at the same time, and which is more specifically literary criticism, *Racine et Shakespeare,* was accepted immediately and brought Stendhal's name before the strictly literary public in Paris. When a bit later Mérimée and Sainte-Beuve commented on his first pamphlet, published in 1823, they referred to the leading concepts and formulas of the tract. The main thesis was the pressing need for a new kind of play in France. The form of classical tragedy has had its day. The alexandrine line was suitable for Racine, but was no longer suitable for the nineteenth-century playwrights. The unity of time, with the action of a play limited to twenty-four hours, as observed by Corneille and Racine, was ludicrous for the contemporary playwrights. In essence, the new playwright has to decide whether he is going to give the maximum pleasure to the audience of his day or to his great grandparents.

Shakespeare is proposed by Stendhal as a new model for French playwrights. And in effect, the plays of Victor Hugo and Alfred de Musset will owe something of their dramaturgy to Shakespeare. The year before the writing of this pamphlet, a company of English actors had performed several Shakespeare tragedies in Paris: *Othello, Richard III, Romeo and Juliet, Macbeth, Hamlet.* But they were not well received and probably for political reasons. The English were held responsible for Napoleon's death in 1821.

The fifty-five pages of *Racine et Shakespeare,* part I, destined to bring fame to Stendhal in literary circles, were largely inspired by the Italian romantic movement, *il romanticismo,* which Stendhal had observed closely and with great sympathy between the years 1814 and 1821. *Il romanticismo* had been more patriotic and more liberal than French romanticism. It had called for literary works celebrating a national liberation, based on Italian themes and freed from traditional rules. Stendhal in both parts of his *Racine et Shakespeare* (the second pamphlet was published in 1825) advocated modernism in art and letters as well as politics, and specifically a simplifying of the writer's language and the use of French history in the choice of subject matter.

The preface to *Cromwell,* published by Hugo in 1827, four years after the first part of *Racine et Shakespeare,* will serve as the principal manifesto of romanticism in France and provide a plan for what Hugo will call the new type of play, *le drame.* But Hugo was preceded by Stendhal, who showed himself in 1823 and 1825 as an innovator in literary doctrine and as a protagonist in the quarrel between the young romantics and the older classicists. Largely from Italian romanticism, Stendhal inherited his general conviction that the writer is the interpreter of his time by composing new works, not based upon rules governing the art of an earlier age. Beauty is not an absolute. It is relative and evolves from century to century. Stendhal takes sides with Shakespeare—who would appear as an innovator for French playwrights in 1825—as against Racine, with Byron as against Boileau. He is opposed not to the tragedies of Racine but to the poetics of Racine and the pseudoclassicism of the 1820s.

Racine et Shakespeare is the most important book of Stendhal in which he expressed the literary ideas of his maturity. It stresses the writer's need to adapt himself to the customs of the day in which he is writing and for which he should write. In the literary skirmishes of Italian romanticism he had observed in Milan, he had become familiar with the works of the poet Monti, of Silvio Pellico (whose *Le mie prigioni* strongly influenced him), of Foscolo, Leopardi, Manzoni. On his return to Paris in 1821, he had an extensive knowledge of the new Italian literature, which was largely unknown to the members of the Paris literary circles. There, in conversations, first, he discussed his theories. His book on *Racine et Shakespeare* was first delivered orally in the *cénacles* and salons of Paris. He deliberately used the Italian form of the term, *romanticismo*, rather than the French form *romantisme*. It is a paradox that Stendhal is in the avant-garde of the romantic movement, because he detested the real founders of the movement, Chateaubriand and Mme. de Staël, and had expressed very slight approval of the prime movers in the 1820s: Hugo, Vigny and Charles Nodier.

The critical concepts in *Racine et Shakespeare* will be recast and clarified and developed by three critics in par-

ticular who occupy a more important place in French literary criticism than Stendhal: Sainte-Beuve, Baudelaire and
Taine. Stendhal's striking definition of romanticism as representing what is modern: *le romantisme c'est ce qui nous est
contemporain*, will be the basis for Baudelaire's more
famous definition which makes a similar claim.

French literary theory in the 1820s did center almost
exclusively on possible reforms in the writing of tragedy,
and here Stendhal's role was significant. The rule of the
three unities was attacked. Stendhal explicitly excludes the
unities of place and time but does advocate maintaining
the unity of action. He defines the pleasure to be derived
by an audience from the performance of a serious play as
that of being absorbed by the action on the stage and by the
experience of living with the characters. Such moments of
participation Stendhal claims are more often to be found
in the works of Shakespeare than in Racine's. In the classical
writer's concern with a unity of tone, he keeps the genres
separated, but the new drama must depict all aspects of
life. Strict demarcations between the genres will have to
disappear. In discussing the French playwright's need to
imitate foreign literatures, Standhal suggests the art of
Shakespeare as the ideal to take as a model, although he
never explains exactly what that art is.

Such a plan, as advocated by Stendhal, would mean a
widening of the scope of tragedy, and this quite specifically
did take place after 1827, after the publication of the preface
of *Cromwell* by Hugo, in which the ideas were not new but
were taken over largely from Mme. de Staël and Stendhal
and expressed more forcefully.

Stendhal as a critic and aesthetician reaffirms the doctrine
of the relativity of beauty. He believes that genres develop,
flourish for a while, and then diminish and exhaust them-

selves. He had grown tired of the typical French tragedy that he saw to be a series of odes interspersed with epic narratives. In recommending dramas in prose based on national subjects, he may well have been thinking of Napoleon. Temperamentally and literarily Stendhal was never a romantic in any strict sense. In his writings he never indulged in sentimentality or in inflated rhetoric. Whenever sentiment is involved in his writing, it has the ring of authenticity and simplicity. He was always perspicacious in his estimates of the sincerity of sentiment and quick to sense any falseness in it, any grandiloquence. In all of his novels Stendhal analyzes strong passions and feelings. His admiration for the deployment of energy is reflected in certain episodes in his writings that often resemble adventure or picaresque novels. But even in such episodes that are farthest from everyday reality, Stendhal brings to his analyses of human behavior under extraordinary circumstances a keen psychological understanding. His style always remains simple and direct. It never imitates the melodramatic actions that are taking place.

Soon after the publication of *Racine et Shakespeare*, Stendhal withdrew from the critical jousts in Paris that centered around Hugo's impressive formulas. Stendhal's search as a writer for psychological and sociological truth led him away from the aspects of romanticism that continued to indulge in a painting of the vagueness and the mysteriousness of man's sentiments and passions in the slow prelude to passions where nothing was clear, in the latter-day development of *le mal du siècle*.

Briefly, then, on his return from Milan in 1821, Stendhal became in Paris the propagandist for a form of romanticism that had little to do with that of Lamartine and Vigny. He was attracted by criticism at that time in his career and published alert and lively critical articles in several English journals between 1822 and 1828. His principal theme was always the question: How can French literature free itself from Louis XIV? He opposed those forces that were holding back the development of literature: the example of the Sun King, l'Académie Française and la Sorbonne. However, this opposition he articulated in a clandestine way by not signing the articles he published in England, did not lead him to an acceptance of Hugo and the more or less organized forces of romanticism. He was disappointed with *Hernani*, and he heaped sarcasm on Vigny's poem *Eloa,* calling it an unbelievable mixture of absurdity and profanation.

IV

Armance

In 1827, at the age of forty-four, Stendhal published his first novel. At the time, it seemed an enigmatic, disconcerting story. The principal theme in the book was so delicately, so chastely developed, that it was not apparent to most of the first readers. And yet this theme had been treated in a novel published a year earlier by Hyacinthe Latouche, *Olivier*, which had caused some degree of scandal on two counts. First, the subject was sexual impotency, and second, it was surmised that Latouche was not the real author of the work.

The Duchesse de Duras, who had published in 1824 and 1825 two successful short novels, *Ourika* and *Edouard*, had written but not published a third story, *Olivier ou le secret*. The rumor spread rapidly in Paris that the "secret" which had forced the hero Olivier to leave the woman he loved was his sexual infirmity. The duchesse had written the work in defiance of the belief—those years of the Restoration were prudish—that such a subject could be treated in a novel.

Latouche finally acknowledged publicly that he was not the author of *Olivier,* published under his name, but that its real author was not the Duchesse de Duras. The mystery of *Olivier*'s paternity has never been cleared up.

In 1826 Stendhal wrote at some length about *Olivier,* in an article published in *The New Monthly Magazine* (January 18), where he praised the work for its originality and attributed its authorship to the Duchesse de Duras. He decided at that time to write an *Olivier* himself, but wisely changed the hero's name to Octave, and gave to the book's title the heroine's name, *Armance.* He was obviously not attracted by the medical aspect of the subject, because his treatment avoids any indulgence in the scabrous. From *Olivier* he retains no details and only, at the most, a vague general plan. The Stendhal work became essentially a description of Paris society. The subtitle is fully justified: *quelques scènes d'un salon de Paris en 1827.*

Stimulated by his reading of *Olivier,* Stendhal began writing *Armance* on January 31, 1826, when he worked on it for nine days, until February 8. There is no reliable reason to explain his interruption of the writing at that time. It may have been the difficulty of the subject, or it may have been personal reasons, the gradual ending of his love affair with the Comtesse Curial. In any case, he was in England, for the third time, between June and September. On his return in the middle of September, the comtesse broke definitively with him, and it is known that Beyle was so desperate over the collapse of this love that he considered suicide. He resumed work on *Armance* September 19 and continued until October 10. These two periods of work, totaling thirty-one days, saw the completion of the novel. He spent very little time revising the work for style. He himself was surprised over the small number of corrections he had to make. The swiftness with which Stendhal wrote all his novels and stories is all the more surprising in *Armance* whose style seems the most carefully and economically composed.

Briefly and superficially, what is the subject of *Armance?* Octave de Malivert has completed his studies at Polytechnique. He is a morose taciturn young man, troubled by some defect in his nature he never discusses, a fairly typical reserved young aristocrat who appears determined not to fall in love. But he is in love, and deeply in love, with his cousin Armance. Because she has no dowry, Armance tries to conceal her love for Octave. Both are noble and overscrupulous young people. Octave in particular is hard on himself. He makes preparations to leave Paris when he is forced to engage in a duel and is seriously wounded. Believing himself close to death, he confesses his love for Armance to her. When he recovers his health, it is impossible for him not to ask her hand in marriage. In the declaration scene, almost as if it were from a Racine tragedy, Octave alludes to some monstrous element of his nature. *Je suis un monstre,* he says at one point. Armance's answer to something she does not fully comprehend is tender and moving. She tells Octave she had contemplated committing a crime that would equal his so that he would cease fearing her.

The marriage ceremony is performed. Although Octave had sworn to take his life in order to liberate immediately his young wife, he is so touched by her love that at first he does not find the courage to commit the deed. But his sense of self-esteem grows. He sets sail for Greece and there on the boat takes poison. The final sentence describing the act is Stendhal at his best. The poignancy comes from the brief notations in each part of the sentence: the midnight scene of the moon rising behind Mount Kalos, the poison clearly designated as a mixture of opium and digitalis and the effect of the poison that cuts off the protagonist from a harassed life:

Et à minuit, le 3 mars, comme la lune se levait derrière le mont Kalos, un mélange d'opium et de digitale préparé par lui, délivra doucement Octave de cette vie qui avait été pour lui si agitée.

In his will, Octave had bequeathed his fortune to Armance on the stipulation that she remarry within two years. We learn that she entered a convent.

The plan of the book is irreproachable in the ordering of the events, in the logic with which every act is carried out. The complications in the story—and there are many of them—arise from the exceptional nobility, the exceptional strength of character in both Octave and Armance. More than the other two far more famous novels of Stendhal, *Armance* is the book of analysis. The subtlety and the finesse of the analyses of *Armance* place it at the head of all the novels of psychological analysis, at least at the head of those in the French tradition.

What forces, what elements concur to make this book an analytical study? First among these forces is Octave's secret that he never divulges but that on two occasions he comes close to doing so. The secret is carefully guarded, but the reader is never allowed to forget that there is a dark ever-present ever-upsetting secret that accounts to a large degree for the strange behavior of the character Octave. He moves back and forth between moments of violence and muteness, between rage and quiet introspection. The need to dissimulate grows into an obsession, and the reader is led to conclude that what is being concealed is some strange

illness, some weakness of which Octave is ashamed. The
obsession over this secret grows more between Stendhal and
the reader than between Octave and Armance. The hero
and the heroine seem to be within their rights in sustaining
a high level of scrupulosity over any expression given to
their most intimate feelings. On another level of scrupulosity, that of the storyteller, a struggle is waged between
Stendhal and his reader over how much is to be revealed
and how much is to be guessed concerning the secret of
the protagonist.

Stendhal chose to focus his attention on the development
of a passionate love in the heart of a type of man who is
referred to in medical language as a *babilan*. The word,
of Italian origin, means a lover who is Platonic because of
his physical nature, because of some physiological defect. It
seems to apply to a man who experiences a very fervent love
for a woman and at the same time a sensual indifference to
her, or a lack of sensual response. This is not an unusual
state of affairs for an idealistic lover. Stendhal himself states
on many occasions in his personal writings that the effusions
of the soul when they are very strong rarely coincide with
comparable desires of the senses. He seems to believe that
in a certain type of man, in Stendhal himself, for example,
the elements of spiritual love and the elements of physical
love tend to be disassociated.

By being an exhaustive and exhausting exhibition of a
man's refinement of feelings, the novel *Armance* is, covertly,
an analysis of a certain kind of sexual frustration. It is also,
on another level, a document on Stendhal's own timidity.
On a still more universal level, it is a study of the demands
that the spirit of a man can make, thereby humbling his
senses and even radically diminishing their power.

Stendhal's reticence in naming Octave's secret is explicable either as further proof of Henri Beyle's personal timidity in such matters or as the novelist's skill at heightening and sustaining the tension in the story's action. There are doubtless elements of both these explanations in *Armance*.

The directness and even coarseness with which Stendhal discusses Octave's *babilanisme* in a now-famous letter to Prosper Mérimée, written on December 23, 1826, should not be looked upon as the sole evidence or even as the most important evidence of Stendhal's convictions about his hero. But at least the letter is far more explicit than the novel is about Octave's infirmity. The letter is obviously a reply to objections raised by Mérimée (to whom Stendhal had shown his manuscript) about the subject matter of the book. The tenor of the letter is the conviction that the number of sexually impotent men is far higher than is usually believed. Stendhal lists ways in which impotency in marital relationships may be offset. The background of the letter is a medical point, which today would find ample justification, that in the case of precocious impotency a man's entire existence is gravely affected. Octave in the novel is obsessed with the fear that he will lose his sanity. In the letter to Mérimée Stendhal refers to the case of Swift, who died insane, and gives evidence of knowing Walter Scott's study of Swift and his analysis of traits in Swift that are also visible in Octave.

Although the tone of Stendhal's letter is cynical, the thesis he defends is familiar enough in real life: the fact that love and the satisfaction of desire do not always coincide. In citing the case of Swift as an illustration of *babilanisme*, Stendhal was not thinking only of a physiological condition that would separate a man from ordinary society and prevent his knowing marital happiness. With the example of *Gulliver's Travels*, he was thinking of a human being placed outside of society, of a civilization, and even of the world, in the situation of a dwarf in a land of giants, or of a giant in a land of dwarfs. This is the situation described in Voltaire's *Micromégas* and in *Les Lettres Persanes* of Montesquieu. The eighteenth century abounds in examples of literary heroes so different from the society in which they live, that they can observe it coldly and judge it.

Stendhal himself was no *babilan*, but he had experienced the disassociation of love and desire, and he had experienced personally the feelings of a man excluded from society by his poverty and excluded from the world in which he had wished to live by the fall of Napoleon's empire. Society in *Armance* is judged by an outsider, by an enemy, as it will be later, in still stronger terms, in *Le Rouge et le Noir*.

The subtlety of Octave's situation comes from all the things that are not said, that are not made explicit. The novel has nothing of a clinical study about it. We have to guess, but with little hesitation, that Octave is not impotent because of some organic malformation. We are led to believe that his body is handsome and strong. There is no trace of infantilism or glandular deficiency or effeminacy about him. He is twenty years old. In his desire to be in the presence of Armance, and at those moments when he is close to her, when he looks at her and at her partially bared breast, when he presses her bare arm, his feelings are those of a man with very normal sexual drives.

The tragic situation of Octave is felt more and more clearly by the reader because of the absence of explicit detail. Octave is not engaged in any recognizable struggle, in any noteworthy effort to move ahead, to progress, to change his life, to defeat his enemy, to overcome an obstacle that can be overcome. He is young, handsome, rich, noble and he is loved by the girl whom he loves. It would be difficult to describe a situation that is more static, that lends itself less to the art of the novelist, that is more prone to bore a reader who thinks of a story as the art of progress, development, peripety, change, defeat or triumph.

For his first novel Stendhal chose a character very much alive, very much in love, and who is suffering from a curse for which he is not responsible. Even if Octave possessed the will and the energy of a Julien Sorel to change his life, there would be no point in it. He has everything from the beginning and no means to enjoy it. The full sense of this starkness is never stated, never described. It is enacted in the final sentence of suicide, and even there no explanation for the fate is offered.

Some of the richest moments of analysis are those when Octave is in the presence of Armance and is drawn to her. Stendhal might have been explicit at those moments, but he refrains always from telling the reader whether this physical closeness pleases or displeases Octave. No sentiment could be as simple as that of pleasure or displeasure, under the circumstances in which Octave finds himself. Even if the reader concludes that Octave's impotency is the result of some neurological cause, no diagnosis is possible because no concrete facts are available.

Whenever a diagnosis is offered, such as that given by André Gide in his very penetrating article on *Armance*, a defect can be found in it by some small action or reaction on the part of Octave. Gide proposes the hypothesis that the cause of Octave's impotence is in a deficiency or a lack of sexual desire. But this could be contradicted by the strong emotion Octave feels when he looks at Armance's *décolletée* and presses her bare arm.

We never learn the physiological explanation of Octave's infirmity, and we never learn the psychological explanation. We read only of the consequences of the mysterious infirmity. The subject matter of the book is the analysis of these consequences that are complex and are studied in minute detail. The exterior behavior of Octave seems to be totally dictated by his malady.

He is in love with Armance, but the idea of loving her horrifies him. He is constantly reminding himself that he has no right to declare his love. The only moment of happiness he experiences is at the time he believes he is going to die and gives himself over to the joy of confessing his love to Armance. At that moment, in speaking of his love, he has no feeling of the shame to come when he will have to confess his infirmity. But prior to that moment of avowal, Octave carefully builds up a reputation of a promiscuous lover and *débauché*. In his frequent appearances at houses of prostitution he hopes to deceive those closest to him in his society, and he is at the same time intent upon testing himself and his own powers. He prefers to give the picture of a *débauché* rather than that of an impotent.

We follow not only the consequences of Octave's defect, but we follow also the result of these consequences on the nervous temperament and complex character of the young man. The elaborate stratagem of social behavior that Octave devises takes its toll on his nervous system. Whatever is physiological in the case of Octave remains a secret. Stendhal quite simply reveals nothing on this subject. But he does reveal, in several scenes, a psychological condition that is complex and serious. To fall in love, as deeply as he does, with such a loving girl as Armance, and then to feel horror at the very idea of loving Armance, and to feel that he can never declare his love are clearly defined situations that justify Octave's temperament and behavior as they are analyzed in *Armance*.

Octave's decision to embark on a voyage to Greece is reached more than half way through the novel. Chapter 20 describes him in Paris preparing for the voyage. It is a moment almost of hallucinations for him. He tries vainly, by talking with his *valet de chambre*, to forget his despair. In the process of packing, everything he handles reminds him of Armance. He knows that Greece is a mirage, that all hope of escaping his suffering is empty. The analysis of this young man walking about his room alone, when he sends his servant out on an errand, is detailed and intense. Even the application of physical pain to himself does no good. The spiritual suffering is far greater than any physical suffering. Intoxication, as night comes on, offers no relief and only enhances a feeling that he is losing his mind. Late at night the silence settling over the house and the land outside gives to Octave, on his balcony looking up at the sky, an even deeper sense of horror for his predicament. When he falls half asleep through extreme fatigue, he is awakened by what he thinks to be the sound of human speech. The next day he tries to forget himself by devious ways: by speaking with his barber or with his servant, by visiting his friend Mme. d'Aumale in her box at the Théâtre Italien.

Octave's obsessions and scruples are pathological. His active intelligence never allows him to stop analyzing himself. Without any close friends, he deliberately alienates those who might be friends. His solitude deepens as his distrust for everyone about him deepens. After swearing he will never fall in love, he goes to the extreme opposite in idolizing Armance, in declaring he cannot live without her.

It is in Chapter 17 that Octave realizes how deeply he is in love, and he describes in an exceptional moment of frenzy the tragic future of this love. The passage begins *J'aime, se dit-il d'une voix étouffée! moi aimer!* . . . A feeling of horror seizes him first. Then he tries to walk in the woods, but has to sit down on the trunk of an old tree. The one sentiment that has guided his life—his self-esteem—he has now lost. Rage overcomes him but he is unable to cry out and thus articulate his rage. As the moments pass, he suffers principally from a loathing of himself. Shame dominates all his feelings, and whatever practical solution occurs to him, such as a possible plan to fight in Greece, he finds it insipid and fatuous.

His suffering reaches such a point that quite literally he loses consciousness: *Octave s'appuya contre un arbre et tomba évanoui.* He recovers when a peasant throws cold water on his face. His thoughts are muddled at first and he cannot recognize the place he is. When he does remember, the presence of the peasant keeps him from giving vent to his anguish. The scene is sober and pathetic, in the best Stendhal tradition.

The confession scene is complex and delicate, because of the tensed nobility of sentiments in Armance and Octave. The physical complications that follow a duel leave Octave in such a condition that he feels close to death and therefore able to reveal to Armance the secret of his life. Moreover, she has just said that they will never be married and that she loves him and him alone. He tells her of the exact moment when he knew that he loved her and then, without revealing the literal truth about himself, lets her believe that he has committed criminal deeds. But this only strengthens Armance's love for him.

Octave is still seeking a solution to his dilemma when a

disreputable character, M. de Soubiranne, invents a letter in which Armance confesses that she loves her cousin only for his fortune. Octave is deceived by the letter and feels he was justified in not revealing his secret (*mon fatal secret*). The novel ends without any scene of explanation between Armance and Octave. He never even reveals the letter. Stendhal, as in a melodrama, allows the reader (spectator) to know the two sides. Octave wills the courage to carry out his last plan and leaves for Greece. On the boat he pretends to be sick and dictates his will in which he obliges Armance to marry within twenty months after his death if she wishes to inherit his fortune. One day at dawn, when the boat is in sight of land, Octave is found unconscious lying on some cordage on the deck. The sailors who help to bury him are struck by his beauty.

The character Octave is the preparatory sketch for *le beylisme*, which will be formulated and developed in *Le Rouge et le Noir*. His death comes about less from his impotency than from his romantic idealism. Julien's ambition will be of a far greater earthiness than Octave's. But the pure sentiment of Stendhal himself that is apparent in Octave will never be totally dissipated by the life of the novelist. And all the major traits of Stendhal's technique are present in the first novel. In claiming that he tried to depict the customs in France during the past two or three years (*J'ai cherché dans ce roman à peindre les moeurs actuelles telles qu'elles sont depuis deux ou trois ans*), he was defining what the novel was for him: his observations of life and customs and his descriptions of them—customs as they were and customs as he saw them in others and in himself. Octave is the younger Stendhal whose violence is less controlled and more feminine than it will be in the subsequent novels. Because Octave is more ambiguous in his soul and in his body, he seems a fictional hero more comprehensible to readers in the 1960s than Julien or Fabrice.

Prior to the writing of *Armance* Stendhal had dreamed only of writing for the stage, and some of the final scenes of the novel might belong to a comedy. At the age of forty-three, to pass from the writing of comedies of character to a novel, a literary form that at that time in France was somewhat looked down upon, was almost equivalent to a defeat. Balzac had not yet made the novel into the supreme literary genre of the nineteenth century. *Armance* is the first novel of manners in the century, the first of a type of novel that will count heavily in prestige by the end of the century. The articles that Stendhal sent to English journals between 1825 and 1826 show the interest he had in the depiction of the French salons characterized by a prevailing melancholy and boredom to which he was sensitive.

The writing of *Armance* marked a change in Stendhal's career. His powers of observation and social criticism were to be used henceforth for novels rather than comedies. He knew that his public for such books would be the social world, and women especially. In the earlier part of his career, he had tried writing biographies, a form of history, and he had become convinced that it was impossible to discover the real truth about a man's life, or at least any detailed truth. Only in the writing of a novel can truth be reached. The interest that had grown up over the novel *Olivier* seemed to Stendhal a legitimate reason for choosing the same subject matter. He had even chosen the name Olivier for his hero, and only changed it to Octave on the firm advice of Mérimée. Many critics have argued that Stendhal was analyzing his own case history in the portrait of Octave. Had he known intermittent periods of impotency caused by emotional tensions and excessive timidity? Both Albert Thibaudet and Paul Morand have pointed out indications that Stendhal had shown definite indulgence for homosexual tendencies in other men. But the letter to Mérimée would seem to indicate that Octave's so-called *babilanisme* was sufficient explanation for the hero's timidity and sense of tragedy. It makes little sense to consider, as some critics have, what a forthright character Octave would be if he were not a *babilan*. If in other characters the Stendhal hero combined love and *espagnolisme*, in Octave he presents the far more special case of a young man in love who suffers from impotency.

The anecdotal origins of *Armance*—its relationship with the works of the Duchesse de Duras and her unpublished story, and with *Olivier* of H. de Latouche—and Stendhal's article about it have little to do with Stendhal's first novel. The subtitle indicates he believed an important function of comedy—the depiction of social manners—was passing into the novel, that the novelist would continue the work of a Molière.

A young aristocrat in love who suffers from sexual impotency would be as worthy a subject for a novel where the social background colors the psychological problem as Molière's Alceste is a suitable subject for a comedy in the seventeenth century where the sincerity of love is heightened as it is played against a frivolous and sophisticated court. The dark secret of Octave and the demanding sincerity of Alceste are obstacles to love. Molière presents his misanthrope with exaggerated comic overtones, whereas Stendhal, in his far more oblique and more slow-moving action, shows a tragic character. Both Alceste and Octave are characterized by neurotic outbursts, and both are deceived by false letters or falsely interpreted letters, which confirm their pessimistic view of society and their fundamental distrust of everyone. The social world of Octave's parents is as skillfully depicted as Célimène's salon. Each salon is the microcosm of the royal court.

Octave is a more modern character than Alceste because he belongs to the later nobility whose most gifted sons were beginning to be educated and think of careers that might remove them from the monotony and indolence of a purely social life. Much importance is attached to Octave's education at Polytechnique. He is a new type of aristocrat under the Restoration who is dissatisfied with the life of idleness and seeking a more useful, a more vital place in the community of men.

The Faubourg Saint-Germain, which Stendhal himself had not frequented, is evoked in the salon scenes and in the characters, not all of whom are necessary to the story. Mme. Bonnivet, protectress of Armance, is characterized by her superficial interest in "religious feeling" (*sentiment religieux*). All the action transpires in the salon, because even in the country, near Paris, the salon is transported there and the same kind of life and the same conversations continue there.

Even when the scenes are essentially those of a salon, the reader is always conscious of Octave's presence in the foreground or background of the salon and of his relationship to it. His social position, his wealth, his manners place him at the center of the Faubourg Saint-Germain, but everything important in his life and in his thoughts drives him outside of the salon. He is not a member of his society. He is excluded from it and not because of his secret, not because of the equivocal drama he refers to and never defines, but because of the admirable nobility and aloofness of his mind. *Armance* is the drama of nobility of spirit, far more than it

is a drama of social satire. The satire is there, either sub-
dued or flagrant, but it is always overshadowed by this figure
who walks about in his own world, just beyond the real
world of Paris society.

In his close scrutiny of himself Octave is aware of his
long line of noble ancestors going back to the crusaders,
of the survival through the centuries of codes of honor and
behavior that explain and justify the severe idealism in
accordance with which he lives. A total lack of complacency
for himself is Octave's leading trait of character, but this
will be true of all the Stendhal heroes. Octave's mystical
ideal of perfection derives from his rank in society. He be-
haves as if he were bound by the vows of a knight templar.
The book could be read by interpreting his secret or his
infirmity as a vow of chastity. The slightest misdemeanor in
such a rigorous code is a falling from grace. In his observations of others, and of course especially of Armance, the
most minute details, the slightest fluctuations are weighed
and judged as if they were acts of virtue or sinful deeds. His
impeccable taste, his aloofness, his rigor place him outside
all the rules of conformity.

In the presentation of Octave de Malivert, Stendhal illustrates as lucidly as in any other literary creation, his method
of composing a character. The social status, first, is clearly
depicted: He is a product of the Faubourg Saint-Germain
between the years 1820 and 1830.

If Octave at one moment frequents prostitutes and at
another moment kills in a duel a fellow of his own age,
these are not the grave matters with which his mind is
occupied. The demands of his sensibility and character
create a drama—it might be called the drama of perfection
—which is a symbolic form of impotency. Octave's scorn for
everything that is low isolates him from ordinary actions

and activities in the world. The coldness of his character, except in his relationships with Armance and his mother, gives an impression not only of detachment but of sterility. In Molière's Alceste there is more fiery opposition to insincerity and dishonesty and hypocrisy, and in Julien Sorel there is more explosiveness, more violence. Alceste is from the bourgeoisie and Julien from the peasantry. The cold courtesy of Octave is aristocratic.

The last four words of the first paragraph in the book, *odieux aux hommes vulgaires*, announce the reaction that most men will have to Octave's overbearing manners. The word *vulgaire* is a leitmotiv in the book. Before Armance falls in love with her cousin, she is obsessed with the question, is his soul commonplace? (*aurait-il une âme vulgaire?*). Until the voyage to Greece at the end Octave never leaves the setting of elegance and refinement that harmonizes with his character. There is nothing of the picaresque hero in him, nothing of the adventurer. We are led to believe that the bordello visits are for the purpose of self-testing and camouflage. The salon in *Armance* is comparable to the palace antichamber in a Racine tragedy or the salon in a classical comedy. There is no need to see the hero in any décor save the one that has helped to form his attitudes and temperament. Octave's inner turmoil is sufficient subject matter for the novelist. He has no need of subjecting his hero to extraneous foreign circumstances.

At the age of twenty Octave is not characterized by acts of revolt against his background or merely by the desire to experience other kinds of life and know people of other conditions. The physical intensity of that age is channeled into a dangerous and exhilarating mode of behavior that is far more rigorous, far more literally observed than the same code followed by others in his family and other families like his own. The usual need for adventure felt by most youths of twenty is converted into the obdurate struggle for perfection in Octave, a Jansenistic application of a way of life, a spiritual battle to subdue anything low or mean or undignified in his mind. He has nothing of the youthful animal-like charm of Julien or Fabrice. His charm is more that of a work of art, of a statue, removed from the ordinary commerce of men. It is the charm of a handsome invulnerability or unapproachableness. Everyone, women and servants alike, forgets that he is still very close to adolescence.

The moments of happiness and enjoyment that Octave experiences in that part of his life we see are so infrequent that they take on a depth and even a pathos that such moments do not habitually provide. The slightest sign, the slightest beginning of happiness becomes for him the source of extraordinary feeling and voluptuousness. The almost trembling approach to happiness—formed by the slightest kind of occurrence, the slightest suggestion—is masterfully drawn by Stendhal. It is in keeping with the paucity of means that he uses in his narrative style. The inflection of Armance's voice or a few of her words overheard are sufficient for Octave to make them into a precious communication. The moment in the woods of Andilly or a summer night when he feels her bare arm against his is one of pure sensation and pure happiness. It is a brief moment shattered by a voice heard in the distance, but the two lovers have come as close to one another at that moment as they ever will. Octave and Armance are cousins and they have the same kind of modesty that is usually called feminine but is also prevalent in a type of young man unpracticed in the concrete arts of seduction. It is not effeminacy but idealism. It is not even timidity, it is a fear of breaking the spell of wonder that surrounds the first certainty of love.

In the second half of the novel there are two distinct moments of a very special kind of happiness that both Octave and Armance experience, the kind of happiness that only a man predestined to suicide, as Octave is, could know.

The first is a moment of reconciliation with the world when they both give up hope in the ultimate kind of love, when they become peacefully reasonable with one another. It is the experience of friendship when seemingly the sexual difference between the man and woman ceases, when Armance becomes the kind of friend Octave never had in his life. Octave announces that he will not marry for six more years, not until he is twenty-six, and Armance lets it be believed that she is promised to someone else. Both of them enjoy the security of friendship without the hope of marriage. Each becomes the confidant of the other. Armance's happiness comes from the full attention she can bestow on Octave, and Octave's happiness comes from a new sense of peace he feels: an absence of anger and a fresh vision of the society about him that no longer seems absurd.

The second moment is more prolonged and more dramatic. Octave's wound is such that it is believed he will not live. Armance comes regularly to his bedside, and there, in an almost mystical way, a kind of marriage is celebrated, comparable to the mystical marriage of Aricie and Hippolyte in Act V of *Phèdre*. Once again, each promises the other to put aside all insistence on a real marriage, and momentarily they enter upon a pact that is both simple and unbinding. The pact is the same as that of friendship, but the feelings of the two cousins are far more intense than they had been previously.

Notations on the beauty of autumn in Andilly accompany this rediscovered sentiment of love. Each confides more deeply in the other. When Octave is allowed to walk outside they rediscover places about which they have memories. These are passages almost comparable to Proustian memories when a relationship between the character and nature is established. Octave grows more indulgent for everyone around him. The entire setting is a preparation for the final confession that is never said. The closest Octave comes to revealing his secret is the phrase: *Je suis un monstre*; and this turns Armance into an even more devoted, more fervent companion. From this point in the story until the end, twenty pages later, the account of pure love—which is now pure passion, in the literal sense of suffering—grows stronger. It is a prolonged love duet, a form of counterpoint where one voice answers the other and vies with it to reach an ever-higher ever-purer tone.

V

Le Rouge et le Noir

THE EARLIEST EMBRYONIC VERSION OF *Le Rouge et le Noir* was a passage in *Promenades dans Rome* on the newspaper story of Laffargue: a cabinetmaker in Bagnères-de-Bigorre who had killed his mistress because of jealousy and who was condemned in 1829 to a five-year term in prison. Stendhal admired Laffargue's expression of violent feelings, claiming they existed only in the lower classes in France. He had also been impressed by the newspaper story of the execution on February 23, 1828, of Antoine Berthet, a seminarian from Grenoble who, in the church of Brangues in Savoie, had shot without killing his benefactress Mme. Michoud de la Tour, because of anger over not having been able to make her his mistress. From this story in particular, Stendhal wrote out the first version of *Le Rouge et le Noir*, in October 1829, and called it *Julien*.

At the beginning of 1830 he was working on some short stories: *Mina de Vanghel, Le Coffre et le Revenant* and *Le Philtre*. In mid-January, he resumed work on *Julien*, on which he spent most of the year. Romain Colomb, his devoted cousin, tells of how one day in May, Stendhal suddenly suggested calling *Julien, Le Rouge et le Noir*. The novelist gave no explanation of the mysterious title to Colomb. The book was printed at the time of the Revolution of 1830. Like Balzac, Stendhal added to his text as he corrected proof which came to him in chapters. It sold fairly well at first, but it seemed to shock Stendhal's literary friends. Mérimée in particular denounced what he called the evil traits in Julien. Balzac spoke of the sinister quality of the book's philosophy and failed to comprehend the complexity of Julien's character. Jules Janin, official critic of *Le Journal des Débats*, and one of the most heeded critics of the day, called Stendhal a skeptic and a scoffer who, because he had no belief in any values, respected nothing and destroyed whatever he touched.

During the first few years after its appearance, almost every commentator on *Le Rouge et le Noir* pointed out the close affiliations between Julien and Stendhal. The novel's hero seemed to be the perfect adept in *beylisme*. This point was made despite the fact that Julien and Stendhal did not belong to the same social class. The difference in historical periods for the two men was more important than the early critics seemed to realize. Henri Beyle was raised during the period of the Revolution and his career was begun during the Empire. Julien Sorel lived at the time of the Restoration, although not long enough to know the July Revolution of 1830. It is not unlikely that had Stendhal written his novel a few months later, he would have portrayed a very different Julien.

The first draft of *Le Rouge et le Noir* has disappeared. There exists a brief notation in Stendhal's handwriting, in the margin of a copy of *Promenades dans Rome*, where the first idea of "Julien" is inscribed: *Nuit du 25 au 26 Octobre, Marseille, je crois, idée de Julien depuis appelé le Rouge et le Noir.* There is disagreement about the year, but it would be one of three: 1827, 1828 or 1829.

When Stendhal undertook the composition of *Le Rouge et le Noir,* he had been writing for thirty years. His program of preparation for the writing of a masterpiece had been meticulously established and carried out: a program of writing every day, of study and of observation. He had studied the philosophers of the eighteenth century and the dramatists of France and Italy. The positions he held in the Napoleonic administration had vantage points for the observation of a variety of human societies. His contacts with groups and individuals and societies had been more extensive than he had ever hoped they would be. His studies of painting and music had accompanied his studies of contemporary society and social customs. He had analyzed the principal passions of man in his book on love. Despite his overwhelming curiosity about social life and his delight in participating in it, and despite his intermittent poverty, he had never neglected his stint of writing a page or two at least every day. The important matter was to write, whether it was a composition of his own invention, or an adaptation, or a translation.

He had practiced his craft for so long in such a varied number of ways that he had become by 1827 the writer, the man who no longer had to heed recipes for writing, who had passed beyond the primitive traps and difficulties of the writer. By the time he began writing *Le Rouge et le Noir,* Stendhal had mastered a style of his own, a swift-moving simple prose, of such total naturalness that often the subtleties of psychological detail escaped his first readers and continue to escape his readers today.

The basis of the narrative is unquestionably the murder (*le crime passionnel*) related in *La Gazette des Tribunaux* during the last four days of 1827. Stories of tribunals, prisons, convicts and gallows were to fascinate not only Stendhal but Balzac and Hugo. The young seminarian Antoine Berthet came from Stendhal's own province of Le Dauphiné. He was sentenced to death and executed because he had shot a lady of the upper bourgeoisie, in whose house he had been employed as a tutor. Berthet exemplified for Stendhal the ardor, the will power and the drive (*énergie*) of a young man from the poorer class in France at the time of the Restoration.

The existence of such an obvious source as this *fait divers* is not as important as the manner in which it is used by Stendhal. The genius of this writer has little to do with inventiveness. He is a master in the unfolding of a story that originated not with him but somewhere else. So, the story of a criminal lawsuit provided the necessary foundation for *Le Rouge et le Noir*. With the outline of such a story clear in his head, the actual writing was not difficult for Stendhal. Ideas about and for the story came into his mind swiftly and profusely. He was so besieged by these ideas that he had to write them out. He imagined that a poet must be obsessed in the same way by the form of his lines.

It was impossible for Stendhal to write in accordance with a detailed outline or with a plan he had considered for some time and had carefully nurtured. The general plan existed fleetingly in his mind and was then discarded or forgotten as he began writing the details he felt an urgent need to consign to paper. Once losing himself in the mass of details, he ceased bothering about the general direction of the book. He seems to have given some heed, in his general preparation for a novel, to the characters. He had fixed in his mind the characterizations: *arrêter les caractères bien nettement.*

For Stendhal's method of writing, it is far easier to work on a story that already exists in some form. Whatever truth emerges from the book would not be history but the precision of details. This is a cardinal belief of Stendhal the novelist. The truth about the human race is not in history, precisely because history does not allow that proliferation or profusion of small details that form the basis for truth in the art of the novelist.

The art of Stendhal, of which *Le Rouge et le Noir* is the supreme example, lends itself generously to the research of scholars, because of the multiplicity of sources that can be detected in a single chapter of his novel, and even on a single page. Everything in the personal experience of Stendhal was utilized in his work: his readings, conversations he remembered, plays and operas he attended, encounters with people, flirtations, street scenes, all the countless observations made verbally or mentally throughout his life. A chapter in Stendhal is a confluence of many elements meeting and mingling to form a unified composition. No one element dominates the other, but each one lends its firmness and coloration to the whole, which is nothing less than a man's biography, his culture and his subconscious life. Stendhal's craft is improvisation, expertly controlled by the excitement of the moment when he is writing. From the mass of sentiments and ideas and details that pass through his mind as he writes, he chooses the clearest and the simplest, those phrases the least charged with poetry. Each phrase is a bare communication, rhythmically sturdy. It is never something added to what has already been written down, in the manner of a Proust.

This archsimplicity of tone and style is offset by the constant presence on his pages of Stendhal himself who remains steadfastly the narrator and whose personality is at all times as interesting as that of his characters. Stendhal is not only in his characters, in Octave, in Julien and in Fabrice, but he is also there purely as himself when he is watching Octave and Armance together, or Julien and Mathilde, or Fabrice and Gina. The bond between author and creature is so close, so acceptable from the very beginning of the story, that the reader, rather than being harassed by this principle of doubling, is intrigued and finally captivated by it. The narrator Stendhal is also the hero of his narration.

The complex problem of sources in Stendhal is related to this function of the novelist as procreator of himself in his heroes. Objective data, such as the details of the *procès Berthet*, have to encounter in Stendhal's mind an early personal memory. Thereby his mind is enriched and stimulated. A personal emotion is renewed and heightened by objective data. Julien Sorel is a transformation of Antoine Berthet and young Henri Beyle, idealized physically and endowed with firmness of conviction, with exceptional powers of memory, with a determination to develop parts of his character that he tests and progressively strengthens.

The letters of Antoine Berthet, and the statements made by him and recorded at the time of the lawsuit, reveal a character quite different from Julien Sorel. He was generally dissatisfied as a child but easily won over by one enticement after another. He exploited his innate weaknesses in order to be helped and praised. He worried over his choice of a religious vocation. He contemplated suicide as often as he contemplated committing crimes. His religious faith was his one solace during the criminal proceedings. . . . The forcefulness and strength of Julien's character must have come from some other source. Stendhal's reading of *Le Mémorial de Sainte-Hélène* undoubtedly provided some of this vigor. Julien himself, in the novel, draws upon the inspiration of this book. The heroics of his character are generously patterned on the example and the figure of Napoleon. The genius of Napoleon, as it is delineated in *Le Mémorial*, encouraged Henri Beyle to live and think as he did, and it likewise encouraged Stendhal's character Julien to grow in accordance with certain of his traits.

The sources of the characters are so many that the danger has always been to make of *Le Rouge et le Noir* a *roman à clef*. Stendhal experts have ascribed to almost every character in the novel the name of a real person, but such coincidences seem to be so rarely deliberate and so often improvised on the spot that the book never appears as autobiography. However, Stendhal demonstrates such a warm sympathy for Julien that the hero seems at least to be a projection of the novelist.

If resemblances are numerous between Julien Sorel and Henri Beyle, contradictions and differences between them also exist. In common they have a hatred for their father and an abiding devotion to their mother who died when they were very young. They both worship Napoleon and cultivate a strong dislike for their native town. Both young men are students of their "philosophy," of their "ideology" (the science of ideas whose genesis and history will explain the world), and draw up careful plans for conquests in life. The seminary, where Julien stands out from the other seminarians, would be somewhat equivalent to the Ecole Centrale de Grenoble. Julien Sorel's arrival in Paris and his employment in the home of the Marquis de la Mole, where his provincial manners become polished, is quite comparable to Henri Beyle's arrival in Paris in 1799 and the protection given to him by his cousin Pierre Daru, the learned statesman and minister of Napoleon.

But even if the liberalism and skepticism of Julien resembles Henri Beyle's, and even if Beyle falls in love as much through vanity as true passion, he remains a civil servant (*fonctionnaire*) and a rather timid lover, whereas Julien's life is characterized by extravagances of conduct. Their beginnings in life were different because of their different social class. At some length, in his final speech to the jurors, prior to his execution, Julien elaborated on his peasant background: *Messieurs, je n'ai point l'honneur d'appartenir à votre classe; vous voyez en moi un paysan qui s'est révolté contre la bassesse de sa fortune.* No originality marked Stendhal's political views. Like most intellectual liberals of his day, who hated anarchy as much as tyranny, he wanted the proletariat to be happy, provided he did not have to live with them.

Napoleon, the artillery lieutenant who became emperor, was the prototype of young Frenchmen about 1830, whose resolute ambition encouraged them to skip the normal stages of social advancement (*brûleurs d'étapes*, they were called). Berthet and Laffargue, by avenging themselves in the same way on the women they loved, bore traits of the type of hero that Stendhal, in his art of novelist, transformed. The village of Brangues, where Berthet shot Mme. Michoud when she was kneeling in church beside her friend Mme. Marigny, will be called Verrières in the novel and moved from La Savoie to La Franche-Comté. Mme. Michoud becomes Mme. de Rênal, and Mme. Marigny becomes Mme. Derville. The plot and the ending of *l'affaire Berthet* do not differ in any essential way from those of *Le Rouge et le Noir*.

The mysterious title of the novel has been explained in various ways, all of which are related to destiny, to the chance that seemed to preside over the significant choices a man has to make in life. Stendhal himself did not speak explicitly on the meaning of his title, but some of his contemporaries believed he meant by "red" the uniform worn in the Revolutionary and the Imperial armies. "Black" would then designate the cassock of the priest. The army and the priesthood were the two possible careers open to a peasant such as Julien Sorel about 1830, especially if he had, exceptionally, the training in Latin that Julien had received. Red and black are also the colors of the roulette wheel. Julien places his bet on the black when he enters the seminary and ultimately loses. At the end of the novel both the executioner and the officiating priest are dressed in black, and there the red would be Julien's blood as it spatters the habit and the uniform of the two men close to him.

In a still bigger sense, the "red" stands for the historical periods of the Revolution and the Empire, for sacrifice and valor, and for the prestige of a military career when action counts more than words, when decisions have to be made quickly, when young men can mount rapidly toward their loftiest ambitions, when physical risks are sources for exaltation, when victory and the dangers that precede victory are reasons for holding on to life. A comparable interpretation for the "black" would be the Restoration and the marked change it represented for the ambitious young Frenchman between 1815 and 1830. There was no chance at that time for military victories and honors earned on the battlefield and swift promotions in rank. All impulses to action had to be restrained. To mount and win favors in the priesthood, to change, for example, the black cassock of a parish priest to the red hat of a cardinal, infinite patience was necessary. The face of holiness is quite different from the face of a conqueror.

Julien first dreamed of electing Napoleon's vocation and then for expediency's sake chose the priesthood. But the more intoxicating dreams of military glory never disappeared completely. In a very dramatic moment, when he was half-concealed, he spied on a young bishop, dressed in processional cope, as he practiced before a tall mirror the gestures of blessing a crowd. The spiritual power in the signs of the cross that the young prelate made alone, as he watched himself, renew in Julien the hopes for a high ecclesiastical position. But he has also in his mind, as he observed the bishop, the more courageous gestures of a young general brandishing his sword over the heads of his men. The political-sociological dramas of two historical periods are in Julien Sorel, and the simple words "red" and "black" symbolize the oppositions and the contrasts characterizing the Empire and the Restoration. But the novel is also the struggle in the heart of a young man over ambition and love—over ambition, designated in the black cloth of the clergy, and over love, whose passion is symbolized by red. Politics is the background for *Le Rouge et le Noir*, as it is for *Armance*, but the psychological drama that this background helps to create, is more centrally captivating for the reader of Stendhal than Henri Beyle's abhorrence for a given régime under the domination of royalists, Jesuits and the enriched bourgeoisie. The historical picture, the ensemble of a Stendhal novel, is powerfully depicted, without any use of large fresco paintings such as we have in Hugo's *Notre Dame de Paris*, published in 1831, a year after *Le Rouge et le Noir*. The reader is never allowed to leave the intricate labyrinth of details, each one of which adds something to the psychological drama. The tenseness of Julien's character and the attentiveness of his mind gradually form into the central drama, but everything else in the story helps to create the tenseness or becomes the object of the attentiveness.

1 · Verrières

Verrières, the first setting of the novel's action, is fictitious. It is a small town of La Franche-Comté, situated on the Doubs River, not far from Besançon. Stendhal presents it as a typical town whose social life feeds on gossip and envy. Under the reign of Charles X and the elaborate spy system of the Congrégation, jealousies and machinations between leading citizens had become more flagrant than ever. The royalists were not only opposed to the liberals, but they were fighting among themselves for promotions and honors.

The novel opens on this sordid political note. The mayor of Verrières, M. de Rênal, who owes his position to the Restoration of 1815, is at odds with the highly respected parish priest Abbé Chélan who had shown the town's prison and poorhouse to a visiting philanthropist, M. Appert. This gentleman had been recommended for the inspection tour by a distinguished Parisian and benefactor of Verrières, the Marquis de la Mole. The mayor feared a hostile report on the state of the institution would be made and reach some liberal newspaper. But the mayor's bad disposition, which he demonstrates as he walks with his wife, is explained more fully by the long-standing rivalry between himself and the director of the poorhouse, M. Valenod, a man who has made every possible move to attract attention to himself in the town. On the surface, cordiality and politeness exist between the two men, but Rênal knows Valenod to be his principal opponent for the mayor's post. The pair of Norman horses which Valenod has just bought and which are admired and talked about is a significant sign for the mayor. He has decided to offset this ostentatiousness by choosing a private tutor for his children and thereby dazzling Valenod and the community of Verrières. This constitutes the opening discussion in *Le Rouge et le Noir*.

Rênal has chosen a young peasant boy, Julien Sorel, highly recommended by Abbé Chélan, and our introduction to him (Chapter 4) is the second development in the novel. Julien's pensiveness, his appearance of almost a young girl, is deceptive. He has the soul and the spirit of a revolutionist. His inner life of reflection and ambition has taken precedence over his exterior life where his family treats him with scorn and looks upon him as a weak and even effeminate outcast.

A retired military surgeon had befriended Julien, had taught him Latin, and bequeathed to him, at his death, thirty to forty books, among which Julien had chosen these favorites: the *Confessions* of Jean-Jacques Rousseau, *Le Mémorial de Sainte-Hélène* and the bulletins of Napoleon's army. From reading such texts as these had come his ambition to better his place in life, to rise in the world as a soldier of Napoleon. But already the time for an Empire adventure had gone by. His only hope now lay in the Church. The priest's black cassock was the new symbol for Julien's liberation, although he was thoroughly convinced of the impostures and mummeries he would have to accept and reenact on entering upon such a vocation. To Abbé Chélan he had already declared his intention to enter the seminary. He had learned the New Testament in Latin by heart.

Chapters 4 and 5 relate the dramatic scene between father and son that takes place in Sorel's sawmill. The aging peasant has struck his son whom he caught reading rather than working, and knocked out of his hand *Le Mémorial de Sainte-Hélène* which fell into the stream flowing through the mill. When the father announced the new post of tutor (*précepteur des enfants*), the boy, whose first thought was that he may be considered a servant, asked with whom he would eat. Reassured that he would eat with the family, he thought instantly of the beautiful house he would see. The details of the treaty are made out by Sorel *père* and the mayor.

The third principal scene is the meeting between Julien and Mme. de Rênal (Chapter 6). It is the classical encounter of the adolescent boy and the somewhat older attractive woman destined to be both mother and mistress. It is Cherubino in the presence of the countess, or Jean-Jacques Rousseau in the presence of Mme. de Warens. At this point, Mme. de Rênal was thinking exclusively of the welfare of her three children. Julien's youthfulness and gentleness reassured her. He would not beat her sons, he would be their friend.

Thus, a new life began for Julien. His newly tailored black suit delighted him because it gave him almost the appearance of a priest. And the first evening in the house, in the presence of the family and servants, he proved his knowledge of Latin and the Bible by reciting from memory passages of which the first words are read to him by his new pupils. Julien was a new discovery for Verrières. His father and brothers were relieved to have him out of the house. M. de Rênal's vanity was flattered to have a resident private tutor. Mme. de Rênal was pleased that her sons would have a companion-tutor. Even her maid Elisa found the household more attractive with the addition of the "pretty little boy-priest" (*le joli petit prêtre*).

With these three scenes, each in turn dominated by the mayor, the father and the young wife-mother, the stage is set for Julien's drama to unfold. It is a drama of pride and endless traces of the susceptibility that had been nurtured throughout his childhood. Every increase of salary and every sign of attention from M. de Rênal would be felt by Julien as a humiliation. His three pupils demonstrated affection for him. His reactions to the boys reveal Julien's inner struggle. He was touched by their signs of affection and wanted to reciprocate, but the happiness and the good fortune of his young pupils reminded him of his own wretched childhood. Instinctively he turned against all manifestations of bourgeois opulence and of easily won contentment.

He nurtured rancor and envy, but learned to conceal them. His sole preoccupation was his ambition to rise in the world and to realize this everything he would do must have a motive pointing toward that goal. The one difficulty in his way, the unpredictable force that could threaten his basic plan, was Mme. de Rênal and the place she began to occupy in his life and in his thoughts.

One summer evening at Vergy, outside of Verrières, where she and her friend Mme. Derville and Julien were talking under a large plane tree, Julien's hand touched hers. The following evening, under the same circumstances, he held her hand. Fundamentally Julien hated Mme. de Rênal because she was rich and beautiful, and he dreaded being caught, as in a trap, by her beauty. Holding her hand was a revenge over M. de Rênal. The following day he escaped to the wood between Vergy and Verrières, and there, on a high rock, watched in the sky the circling of a hawk: *Quelque épervier . . . décrivant en silence ses cercles immenses.* How he envied the strength of the bird and its aloneness! *. . . il enviait cette force, il enviait cet isolement.* The hawk reminded him of Napoleon's destiny and he wondered if one day he would know the same destiny: *C'était la destinée de Napoléon; serait-ce un jour la sienne?* (Chapter 10).

The seduction continued that very evening. When night fell, Julien seized the half-bare arm of Mme. de Rênal and covered it with kisses. He wrote down the plans for his "campaign," as he called it, and announced to her that he will come to her room at two in the morning. Although choking with fear, he did go into her room and made love to her. Throughout the scene, and in spite of the moments of passion and pleasure, he never forgot his role of conqueror. He refused to accept a simple kind of happiness through fear of appearing ridiculous in his inexperience. On returning to his room, he reviewed every step of the seduction and asked himself: Is that what is meant by being loved by a woman? *être heureux, être aimé, n'est-ce que cela?* (Chapter 15).

Months went by. Verrières was stirred by the announced visit of a king (never named by Stendhal) who was coming to pray before a relic of Saint Clément in the neighboring town of Bray-le-Haut. The sons of the best families hoped to belong to the guard of honor. The Marquis de la Mole was coming from Paris for the occasion. His friend Abbé Chélan had been relieved of his pastorate in Verrières, and the mayor was worried about the marquis' reaction if his old friend the priest had no part in the religious ceremonies. Abbé Chélan was finally invited to participate and to have as his subdeacon his former pupil Julien Sorel. This came about through the insistence and the intrigues of M. de Rênal, while at the same time Mme. de Rênal secured for Julien a place in the guard of honor, which meant having a blue uniform made to order and hiring a horse for the young man.

The day was radiant and full for Julien. A few hours

after parading in a dazzling uniform on horseback, he was dressed in his deacon's surplice, beside Abbé Chélan and very close to an extremely young bishop whose mitre shone in the sunlight. The young bishop was the nephew of M. de la Mole, who had only recently been elevated to the small bishopric of Agde in Le Languedoc. He had been chosen to show the relic to the king during the ceremonies. At one moment earlier in the day the bishop had disappeared. Julien, who was wandering through the abbey, found himself in a large room at the end of which he saw a full-length movable mirror. There he watched, unseen at first, the young bishop making signs of the cross in front of the mirror. He was practicing for the ceremonies! Julien was struck by the youthfulness of the bishop, by his gracefulness, by his vanity. The bishop, with marked politeness, as if he were pleased by the intruder and Julien's appearance, sent the boy to get his mitre.

The sparrow hawk over the forest of Vergy had reminded Julien of Napoleon. The young bishop of Agde in the abbey of Bray-le-Haut reminded him of his ecclesiastical ambitions. He forgot Napoleon and he forgot Mme. de Rênal as he watched the young bishop giving benedictions in front of the mirror.

Abbé Chélan who, from Elisa, had learned of the liaison, called Julien to his lodging and demanded that the fellow leave in three days for the seminary in Besançon. Julien yielded not only because the old priest exerted considerable power over him, but also because the Rênal situation had become impossible. During the farewell scene (Chapter 23) Mme. de Rênal who believed she was saying good-bye forever to Julien, became cold and insensitive. Her kisses were without warmth and Julien was strangely upset.

2 · The Seminary

Everything horrified Julien in the seminary: the mute black-robed figure who let him in and showed him the way to the seminary director, Abbé Pirard, the long wait before the priest recognized his presence, and the first exchange of words. A long conversation in Latin was convincing proof to the priest of Julien's intelligence, and the boy was accepted as a seminarian.

Abbé Pirard recognized the worth of Julien and appointed him assistant teacher of the New and Old Testaments. But this priest's position became unbearable in the seminary because of the hostility toward him of high prelates in the diocese, and he ended by accepting the post of a parish outside of Paris. In order to rescue Julien from the seminary, he recommended him as a secretary to his friend M. de la Mole. This appointment to Paris marked the third change in Julien's career.

Before going to Paris, and despite Abbé Chélan's order to see no one in Verrières, Julien one night climbed a ladder to Mme. de Rênal's room and spent several hours with her. A dispute at the beginning of this meeting was followed by a reconciliation. But in order to make love to her, Julien had to argue for so long and use such artifice, that the passion he had felt on entering her room, had diminished into a mild form of pleasure. Mme. de Rênal concealed Julien one more day in the house, but his presence was discovered by M. de Rênal. On escaping from the house the second night, Julien was shot at by the servants.

3 · Hôtel de la Mole (Book II)

On arriving in Paris, Julien's first action was to visit Malmaison, in memory of Napoleon, and to renew in himself the source of strength that the emperor's image always gave him. Then he called on Abbé Pirard who spoke to him in detail about the de Mole family and about what his functions of secretary would be. The priest called the marquis one of the great nobles of France, *un des plus grands seigneurs de France* (Chapter 1). His wife was described as haughty but polite and totally insignificant as a character. The son, Comte Norbert, age nineteen, had been a courageous soldier in Spain, was a dandy in his dress, witty in his speech, and somewhat spoiled by life. The priest pointed out the marquis' hope that Julien would become a friend of his son. He did not speak of the daughter Mathilde, except to say there was a daughter in the family. Julien's principal work would be the writing of innumerable letters having to do with lawsuits. The priest urged Julien to continue his studies of theology by attending a seminary three times a week. If the household became unbearable for Julien, Abbé Pirard offered him the post of vicar in his parish and thereby promised to look after him. Tears came to his eyes when Julien heard these words. He confessed that the calamity of his life had been the hatred he had felt from childhood for his father, but that in Abbé Pirard he had found a father: *j'ai retrouvé un père en vous, monsieur.*

The five pages of this conversation conclude the first chapter of the second book. They recapitulate and deepen the principal drama of Julien Sorel's life. They prepare, by the information they provide, the specific drama of the second book, which will unfold in the Hôtel de la Mole. They add prodigiously, by means of subtle and characteristic traits of Stendhal's art, to the reader's understanding of Julien Sorel and of his relationship to other human beings, especially to the father image.

The scene begins and ends with Julien weeping. At La

Malmaison he wept. There, invisible, the supreme father-image of Napoleon caused such strong emotion (*transports*) in Julien that he broke down in tears. Such was the intensity of his feelings that Stendhal the novelist, intervening directly in his narrative, says he cannot relate the emotions as they were expressed. Julien's devotion to Napoleon would seem to be the most sacred of all, the ineffable devotion.

In the presence of the priestly father, Julien was at first sensitive to the coldness of Abbé Pirard's speech, to the tone of his factual analysis of the de Mole family and to the very swiftly said but very pointed and useful advice given to Julien. As a father should, he prepared the son for the difficulties of life ahead.

In a general way Julien was already convinced that Paris was a seat of perdition and the very heart of intrigue and hypocrisy. He did not admire the Paris of the living, but only the monuments of Napoleon.

For Julien's enlightenment, Abbé Pirard analyzed the de Mole family as if it were the microcosm of French aristocracy and the world itself that would have to be understood before it could be invaded and seduced by a member of the proletariat. From the four members of the family, the priest chose the son Norbert to discuss somewhat in detail, as best representing the family in its relationship to all the possible difficulties facing Julien as he began working for the marquis and living in the same house with the family. Norbert was described as a young nobleman, believing in the superiority of his class, scornful of inferiors, a mocker underneath a façade of wit and politeness, courageous in battle, aware that he was destined to become a peer of France. Abbé Pirard warned Julien that Norbert might cause him the deepest distress.

M. de la Mole was fundamentally a pious humanist. He

respected the clergy, especially such a priest as Abbé Pirard who obviously possessed the quality of uprightness and such an able Latinist as Julien who might be destined for the priesthood. He therefore looked upon the *abbé* and the young secretary as human beings who were cultivated in their own way. Mme. de la Mole looked upon them as priests who were merely indispensable for her salvation (*elle nous considère comme des valets de chambre nécessaires à son salut*).

At the end of this history of possible difficulties, Julien was not totally unaware of the priest's struggle with himself not to love Julien too much. At the same time each one, the older and the younger man, was striving to conceal the love he felt for the other, a love that would be characterized by them as paternal and filial.

The library, which was to be Julien's domain, delighted him. The discovery of the eighty volumes of an edition of Voltaire, in handsome binding, raised his spirits. But the marquis caught a misspelling in the first letters copied by Julien: *cela* written with two l's, *cella*.

The first evening he was introduced in the salon to Mme. de la Mole who hardly deigned to look at him at the beginning. But by the end of the dinner she did look at him with more favor because he had been able to hold his own in a conversation about the Latin poets and about Rome. Mme. la marquise approved of anyone able to amuse her husband. Julien's knowledge of Horace had once served him well in a conversation with the bishop of Besançon, and from that conversation he had remembered certain ideas about the Latin poets, which he brought into his first dinner conversation at the de Moles. His initial victory at the Hôtel de la Mole was won through Latin, and he had impressed the Rênal household by the same means two and a half years earlier. Some of the other dinner guests, especially a well-informed *académicien des Inscriptions*, referred to modern names, such as Southey and Lord Byron, and there Julien was at a loss. But he was accepted as a promising Latin humanist despite his spelling mistakes in French, which the marquis announced to all.

We follow this initiation to a sophisticated Paris world, a scene swiftly described in only four pages, and then at the same time we see various members of the group through the eyes of Julien. Each notation is brief but meaningful. The first person Julien noticed was the young bishop of Agde who had spoken to him a few months earlier at the ceremony of Bray-le-Haut. But the prelate, aware of Julien's pleasure at seeing him, deliberately did not recognize him. How many things are said and concealed in the simple statement: *le jeune prélat . . . ne se soucia point de reconnaître ce provincial* (Chapter 2)! Such a sentence, in true Stendhalian style, contains and conceals at the same time the rich ambiguities of the young bishop's social fears and personal fears.

The third chapter (*Les premiers pas*), which narrates Julien's second and third days at the Hôtel de la Mole, is even richer in its notations and revelations. Count Norbert came to the library "to study" a newspaper in order to be able to discuss politics in the evening and was pleased to find Julien whose existence he had forgotten. In one sentence Stendhal recapitulates and deepens the traits of young Norbert de la Mole. One does not "study" a newspaper, unless one's intelligence is fairly limited. And to forget the existence of a man seen the night before is proof of how little a Julien Sorel would count in the life of a nobleman such as Norbert . . . *il venait étudier un journal, pour pouvoir*

*parler politique le soir, et fut bien aise de rencontrer Julien,
dont il avait oublié l'existence.*

Norbert's invitation to Julien to go riding with him was
expressed in a totally felicitous way: "My father has liber-
ated us until dinner time" (*Mon père nous donne congé
jusqu'au dîner*). Julien was seduced by the *nous*. He an-
swered with equal ingenuousness and politeness by saying
he had ridden horseback only six times in his life. "So, this
will be the seventh," was Norbert's reply. Norbert has the
manners of a gentleman and of a friend, even if he has to
"study" the newspaper. On the return ride, Julien fell from
his horse into the mud of the rue du Bac. When at dinner,
the marquis asked about the ride, Norbert in his reply
avoided any mention of Julien's accident, but Julien immediately confessed his awkwardness by saying there had
been no way by which the count could have tied him to the
horse. The laughter of Mlle. Mathilde and the amazement
of the marquis and the others that Julien, before ladies,
would confess to his riding disaster were signs of the young
man's success. Mathilde looked more searchingly into the
eyes of her father's secretary. By the end of the evening the
three young people talked freely among themselves and
laughed, as if they were equals and had known one another
all their lives.

The scene is essentially Julien's. His relationship with
each of the other three characters is that of a subordinate
who is just beginning to feel a bit at ease in the Hôtel de la
Mole. The entire episode—from the morning encounter
with Norbert, through the afternoon ride, to the dinner and
into the post-dinner conversation—is a social test on many
levels for this boy from the peasant class. His instinctive
good taste, his feelings of pride and dignity, his wit, which is
related to his frankness, ingratiate Julien to all those in his

new setting and assure for him a position which will grow in importance. He was both diplomat and charmer. He used adroitly his unexpected mud bath in the middle of the rue du Bac.

This spotting of mud is a Stendhal theme of humiliation. It is in *Lucien Leuwen*, when Lucien, at Blois, opens his carriage door and a shovelful of mud falls on his face. It is in Stendhal's personal writings when he speaks of often falling from a horse and being humiliated before the grooms. It is, in a word, a Don Quixote theme, utilized by Stendhal to characterize the nonheroic hero, to point up in him the fear that a seemingly heroic gesture will appear ludicrous.

As the months went by Julien turned against everyone: the guests, Count Norbert and Mathilde. But the Marquis de la Mole's attachment to Julien deepened. The boy's intelligence impressed him more and more, and he began to entrust more difficult matters to him. The marquis had a blue suit made for Julien and began pretending that he was the son of a duke, an old friend of the marquis. From then on, when Julien wore his black suit he was treated as a subordinate, but when he wore his blue suit in the evening he was treated as an equal. A quasifrankness grew up between the older man and his young friend. Julien concealed only two matters from the marquis: his admiration for Napoleon and his skepticism (*incrédulité*) in religion, which would not appear suitable for a future priest. M. de la Mole was both father and teacher. Whenever he felt ashamed of his attachment to Julien, he would excuse it by comparing it to a man's love for his dog.

With Chapter 8, Mlle. de la Mole begins to occupy a more important place in the narrative. She and her mother returned from some months in Hyères, an island in the Mediterranean, off the coast of Provence. She found Julien changed. He was taller, paler, and had lost his provincial traits. He treated her with aloofness, and she responded with equal coolness by ordering him to attend the ball given by the Duc de Retz. There Julien met a friend of Abbé Pirard, Count Altamira, a Neapolitan whose liberal views pleased him, and who shared with Julien the same scorn for the society of their age. At one moment in the evening, Mathilde easily overheard Julien praising Danton, and the next day in the library she found him still agitated over the political concepts of Danton and Mirabeau. With marked indiscretion she asked Julien what had turned him into a kind of Michelangelo prophet: *Qu'est-ce qui a pu faire de vous une espèce de prophète de Michel-Ange?* (Chapter 9).

That evening at dinner, Mathilde was the only one dressed in mourning. Julien asked the academician for an explanation. The date was April 30. Mathilde dressed in black because on that day in 1574, on the Place de Grève, the lover of Marguerite de Navarre, Boniface de la Mole, was decapitated for having tried to liberate princes emprisoned by Catherine de Médicis. Mathilde, whose full name was Mathilde-Marguerite, had told the academician that the part of the story which moved her the most was the request of Marguerite de Navarre, addressed to the executioner, for the head of her lover. The night following the execution the Queen took her lover's head with her in a carriage to Montmartre and buried it herself in a chapel at the foot of the hill.

This story was a turning point in Julien's opinion of Mathilde. He found in her a counterpart of himself. Her cult for Boniface de la Mole and her admiration for the entire sixteenth century and its violence paralleled Julien's cult for Napoleon and for the achievements of the Corsican soldier in Europe. Julien and Mathilde are alike in their

suspicions of one another, and they change easily from marks
of extreme friendliness to feelings of hostility. He is fascinated by her spirit, by the books she reads, by her beauty,
by her revolt against the conventionality of her world and
her refusal to take seriously the mild courteous suitor for
her hand, the Marquis de Croisenois. When she leans on his
arm (as once Mme. de Rênal had done), he wonders if she
wants him: *serait-il vrai qu'elle a du goût pour moi?* (Chapter 10). He argues back and forth with himself that either
she is making a fool of him or that she is wooing him (*elle
me fait la cour*). Julien's fear of being humiliated or tricked
is as intense as his desire to attract and even to conquer this
proud girl who seems to rule the family. Since he is a
plebeian, his love for Mathilde, if it is love, will have to
be a conquest. To fall in love with the wrong person, as
judged by the world, is an intoxicating challenge for both
Mathilde and Julien.

By announcing his departure for Le bas Languedoc to
examine property of the marquis, Julien drew from Mathilde a declaration of love. He savored his triumph by contrasting his social position with hers: *moi, pauvre paysan,
j'ai donc une déclaration d'amour d'une grande dame!*
(Chapter 13). Because of Mathilde's letter, Julien imagined
all kinds of machinations against him. He bought a large
Bible, hid the letter in it, and sent it to his friend Fouqué
for safekeeping. One short sentence describing the con-
vulsed features of Julien's face as he imagined plots to get
the letter summarizes the entire story of *Le Rouge et le
Noir*: a wretched man at war with society (*C'était l'homme
malheureux en guerre avec toute la société*).

The next day, after the exchange of more letters, Mathilde
wrote to him to come to her room at one o'clock that night,
by using a ladder. Julien argued with himself that not to go

would be cowardly. In clear moonlight he placed the ladder against the house, and, full of fear, climbed up to Mathilde's room. When he got to the window, it opened and Mathilde told him that she had been watching him below for an hour. *Vous voilà, monsieur, lui dit Mathilde, avec beaucoup d'emotion; je suis vos mouvements depuis une heure* (Chapter 16). Stendhal does not at this point describe any romantic scene. Julien and Mathilde are quite simply embarrassed at the beginning. The anxiety of waiting and the fear of being caught, on the part of Julien, have cooled their ardor. They talk about love, but coldly, and they end by making love for the first time, through a sense of duty. Mathilde was thereby rewarding Julien's bravery, and Julien was curious about the absence of happiness in the scene.

Julien's behavior toward Mathilde was henceforth very much guided by his reading of *Le Mémorial de Sainte-Hélène,* where he studied Napoleon's precept that the best way to subjugate an enemy is to terrify him. Mathilde concurred with Julien's arguments and urged that he dishonor her. Her acceptance of such an act would be a guarantee of her love. His love for her was as intense as hers for him. The drama between them was not one of love but one of temperament. Finally, in an almost haphazard way, she told Julien that she was pregnant. This was the guarantee he needed. She was his forever. *Maintenant douterez-vous de moi? n'est-ce pas une garantie? Je suis votre épouse à jamais* (Chapter 32).

After the expected explosion of anger on the part of M. de la Mole, he compromised generously with the situation by giving Julien a lieutenant's appointment in the *hussards* and a nobleman's title—Julien Sorel de la Vernaye—and sending him to Strasbourg. There was hope that marriage would ultimately be consecrated. But a letter from

Mme. de Rênal to the marquis accused Julien of the worst motivation: the seduction of the principal woman in the household in order to secure a fortune for himself. Mathilde called Julien back from his regiment in Strasbourg and showed him the letter. He left for Verrières where, on his arrival Sunday morning he purchased a pair of pistols, went to the church during mass, stood just behind the bench of Mme. de Rênal, and at the moment of the elevation when her head was lowered, fired two bullets. The first missed her. She fell with the second.

4 · Prison

The fourth and final section of the novel begins with Chapter 36 and occupies ten brief chapters.

Julien was arrested and taken to the Verrières prison. After a night's sleep he confessed his guilt to the judge and wrote a letter to Mathilde in which he urged her to take no one into confidence and after one year to marry M. de Croisenois. The Julien episode in her life will cure her, he says, of the romantic needs of her nature (*le romanesque et le trop aventureux dans votre caractère*).

From his jailer, Julien learned that Mme. de Rênal did not die from the bullet wound and that in fact the wound was slight. He was jubilant over this news although he continued accusing himself of deserving death. Abbé Chélan and his faithful friend Fouqué came to see him in his cell. Fouqué proposed a possible escape from prison but Julien refused. One morning the door of his cell opened abruptly and Mathilde, in the dress of a peasant woman, rushed in. Julien had taken on for her the proportions of the heroic lover of a past age, and she, too, by her behavior wanted to defy society.

When Mathilde was caught up in a plot of intrigue for Julien's liberation, he remained in a state of nostalgia for love and tenderness and mentally made plans for the birth and the care of his child. At the trial, Julien's youthful beauty is described in detail and the effect he had on the women crowding the courtroom. He refused to say a word in his own defense, and his short speech made it impossible not to convict him of attempted murder. To the jurymen he pointed out that he was a peasant in revolt against the limitations of his social position. He expected a just death. His crime had been premeditated and it was against a woman who had been kind and generous to him. He also pointed out that he was being judged not by men of his own class, but by a group of indignant bourgeois.

The death penalty was pronounced immediately. The next day, Mathilde tried to have him sign an appeal, but he refused. Mme. de Rênal came into his cell and confessed that she had been led to write her incriminatory letter by her confessor, Abbé Maslon. Julien was deeply moved at seeing her and said that his love for her was comparable to the love he should feel for God. She implied that she will take her life when Julien is executed. M. de Rênal forbad his wife to pay daily visits to Julien. But Mathilde came regularly, with plans to implore the king for Julien's release and with accusations that he loved his first mistress more than he loved her.

Julien had no desire to be pardoned. His thoughts were fixed on the guillotine, on the hypocrisy of religion as represented by such priests as Frilair and Maslon, on the lack of natural rights for man. His last happiness was that of seeing once more Mme. de Rênal. During the last days of his life, he saw the two women he had loved, and his friend Fouqué. The sun was magnificent on the day of his execution. As he walked outside, the fresh air exhilarated him. He was proud of the courage he felt in himself. Stendhal speaks of the beauty of Julien's head as he walked to his death, and uses the word *poétique* to describe it. The execution was performed with simplicity, and without any trace of affectation. Stendhal's narration is told in equally simple brief terms.

Julien had promised Fouqué two nights earlier that he would not show fear, that he would not turn pale. He had asked Fouqué to drive Mathilde and Mme. de Rênal in the same carriage because he felt that the grief of one would help the other. He had already drawn from Mme. de Rênal a promise that she would care for Mathilde's son. He had asked to be buried in the cave of the mountain overlooking Verrières. It was from the site of that cave that Julien had experienced his strongest feelings of ambition.

There is no description of the execution itself. At the end of the day, Fouqué was alone in his room, with Julien's body. Unexpectedly Mathilde came and asked to see her lover: *Je veux le voir.* She found the strength to uncover the body by thinking of Boniface de la Mole and Marguerite de Navarre. She placed Julien's head on a small marble table and lit some candles around it. She kissed Julien's forehead. The next day she accompanied the casket, Fouqué and a large number of priests to the grave that Julien himself had chosen. On her knees she carried the head of the man she had loved so passionately . . . *elle porta sur ses genoux la tête de l'homme qu'elle avait tant aimé.*

The grotto at the top of the mountain was illuminated with countless candles. Twenty priests celebrated the office of the dead. The unusualness of the ceremony had attracted all the inhabitants of the mountain villages. Mathilde, dressed in deep mourning, walked among them and had thousands of five franc coins distributed. When finally she was alone with Fouqué, she insisted on burying Julien's head with her own hands. Fouqué himself was crazed with grief.

There are at least ten such scenes, poignantly and briefly narrated, which emphasize the dramatic feelings of the characters, scenes that are memorable in the intensity of the purely human dramas with which the story is concerned. They are so vibrant, in the simplicity with which Stendhal relates them, that the reader forgets momentarily that *Le Rouge et le Noir* is pervasively from beginning to end a political novel. The background of the story, France of 1830, cannot be separated from the human dilemmas of Julien and Mathilde, of Fouqué and Mme. de Rênal, of Valenod, the Marquis de la Mole and the Maréchale de Fervacques. There are a few honest people who appear in the book, but the majority of the characters are concerned quite literally with stealing in one form or another and with plots that will elevate them from a lower position to a higher position in the social scale. Venality characterizes every level of society, from the jailor who easily accepts a bribe to a judge who is coerced by the promise of a decoration. Honesty is reprimanded and quickly replaced. Every individual has to be the creature of someone else.

M. de Rênal is a moderate in the new party, and M. Valenod is a militant extremist who will thereby replace de Rênal at the end. In the same way and for the same reasons, the Jesuit Maslon will replace Abbé Chélan. Christian obedience is really political obedience in *Le Rouge et le Noir*. There is no discussion in the seminaries, there is only obedience. The same pattern is evident in the salon of the Marquise de la Mole, where no political problem is ever discussed, where the young men habitués speak of Rossini's music and where academicians discuss the poetry of Horace. From time to time someone coming from Saint-Cloud into the salon merely reports on the king's health.

The deepest political lesson of the book is to be found in the chapter called *La Note Secrète* (Book II, Chapter 21), where Julien is sent abroad to meet some mysterious personage. The French reign is supported by foreign powers. The Jesuits form the foundation of the regime. The seminaries are the schools that train the members of the party. An invasion from abroad is prepared and always possible if there is a weakening in the regime. This is the picture of France of 1830, as told by Stendhal, an opponent of the regime.

The figure of Napoleon is the real clue to *Le Rouge et le Noir*. He is everywhere in the novel because the story of his rise to power is, by 1830, far more than history. It has become the myth that enflames the imagination of Julien Sorel and that explains the political and the social structure of France in which Julien is caught. Whenever Julien refuses what is offered to him, whenever a strong feeling of anger mounts in him, the explanation is to be found in the Napoleonic myth, in the medallion representing the lieutenant of Brienne, a medallion that Julien hides in his straw mattress.

The skill with which Stendhal disguises politics in *Le Rouge et le Noir* is exemplary. But it is there. Stendhal is a propagandist as well as a novelist. In the ball scene of Chapter 9 (Book II), every word exchanged between Julien and Altamira reveals their scorn for the political regime. Altamira, exiled and condemned to death by his country, is for Julien a hero, and like all the heroes of Stendhal, Altamira is best characterized by his power to mock and to scoff.

In the portrait of Julien that Stendhal gives, he paints a tragic hero in the classical sense, a man crushed by his

society, by a force beyond his powers to combat. Julien is a
hero who is defeated and who never accepted the forces that
bring about his defeat. Everything in the book is organized
around this theme. Julien's fate is presented as an accusation
against his age. By his isolation from his own class, Julien is
turned into an enemy of the *bourgeoisie*. He is a servant of
the *bourgeoisie* and he never ceases judging the class he is
forced to serve. Since he never recognizes the morality that
judged him at the end, it is difficult to condemn him. He is
guided by an instinctive sense of nobility that has nothing to
do with the legislative powers of the ruling class. Like
Spartacus, his revolt isolates him and he grows inwardly in
accordance with a personal morality that has no resemblance
to bourgeois morality.

Only on the surface does Julien Sorel appear hypocritical.
He is, in a profound sense, the opposite of the hypocrite. He
is a crusader for a better morality, and he uses hypocrisy as
the only weapon available. His hypocrisy has no feminine
weakness in it. It is aggressive, and it never adulterates the
chivalric intentions of his spirit. He is a peasant in revolt,
the son of a carpenter living at the time of the Restoration,
but he is also the young man of every age who refuses to
submit to the social and political conservatism of his age.

Julien is both a specific portrait of a young Frenchman
and a general portrait of a certain kind of youth. In his
particular characteristics he is distrustful and at times surly.
But he can also feel a sentiment almost of love for young
Count Norbert de la Mole whose perfect politeness protects
him at the dinner on the day he falls from his horse. He has
the prudence of a peasant, but he can also defy and challenge, when the occasion calls for that behavior. He is the
product of his class and also the product of his very special

education. He emulates Napoleon spiritually and mentally. All the episodes of his life are translated into such terms as "skirmishes" and "battles." Every social move is prepared by Julien as if it were a military strategy. We remember that at the conclusion of one of his major "battles" with M. de Rênal, when he sits on a high rock in the woods overlooking Verrières, close to the grotto where in just a few years he will ask to be buried, he watches the circling of a hawk in the sky and likens the bird's fate to Napoleon's. Stendhal, in his marked sympathy for Julien, seems to place the man, defeated by fate, above the figure of the emperor and his dazzling success. The man condemned by society, is higher, in the spiritual sense, than the conqueror.

The action of defeat which fills so much of the actual plot of *Le Rouge et le Noir*, would not be so explicitly tragic without the elaborate analysis of Julien's sensibility of which most of the traits are Stendhal's own. Innately the boy has all the instincts of the aristocrat. Everything that is ugly or base repulses him. Three scenes, among countless others, emphasize this: In the presence of M. de Rênal, Julien feels disgust for the manners of the mayor; at the reception Valenod gives in honor of Julien, the boy is sickened by the traits of vulgarity and egoism around him; at the seminary he is constantly shocked and distressed by what he observes and what he hears. Hundreds of details throughout the book illustrate Julien's delicacy of taste and his instinctive withdrawal from any manifestation of physical or moral ugliness. Julien is fundamentally more noble than he is ambitious. His drives for ambition are all motivated by his desire to live apart from the ugly and the mean.

In the social sense, Julien's native nobility of spirit was made legitimate through the intervention of M. de la Mole when he was elevated to the rank of Julien de la Vernaye and appeared in front of his regiment in Strasbourg, on an excellent horse, and demonstrated the bearing of a nobleman. Stendhal's dream for all of his heroes was the same as the dream for himself. Young Henri Beyle facing the many judges and despots of his life relives in Julien Sorel, in Julien's sensibility, in his peasant's longing for a way of life that would remove him from the coarseness of the atmosphere in which he first lived. Those moments in the youth of Henri Beyle and Julien Sorel when they appeared proud and scornful to others around them were efforts to mask the tears that fell in the solitude of their frustrations.

The young Frenchman from Grenoble and the young hero from Verrières both lived in accordance with the belief that beyond the meanness and vileness of men there must exist a life of happiness. There must be a secret life of happiness that can be reached. *Le Rouge et le Noir* is a novel about the dream of happiness. This premonition of happiness dominates the very early scene in the novel when Julien approaches the Rênal house. As he knocks on the door, his expectancy is as definite as is Mme. de Rênal's surprise a few minutes later when she meets Julien and can hardly believe in her good fortune that the young boy will be her sons' tutor. At that moment, Julien's vision of a beautiful young woman and Mme. de Rênal's vision of a handsome young man are precisely the promise of happiness which is in the warm physical sensations that both of them feel. This momentary sensation of happiness will never be forgotten in the novel. It is the reckless demand of youth that Stendhal articulates and rearticulates in his books. He is the artist in words of man's most insistent dream of happiness and beauty in love. That first moment for Julien was so filled with

promise and light that it was able to sustain him through the
next few years that he was destined to live. A few privileged
moments in his life stand out in stark contrast with the
habitual atmosphere of machinations and human ugliness.
Julien's tears flow easily on those rare occasions when he
experiences human goodness and sympathy. The moments
of emotional crisis, such as the one when Abbé Chélan expresses his friendship for Julien, are far more important in
the development of the boy's character than his moments of
social triumph. He learns more from happiness, usually expressed in tears, than he learns from the paltry unstable
victories over the obdurate selfishness of mankind. Julien's
aptitude for a peaceful and simple happiness is not unlike
Jean-Jacques Rousseau's aptitude for the same kind of happiness. The scene under the linden tree at Vergy, when
Julien holds Mme. de Rênal's hand, is a tactical victory for
him, but it is also the savoring of a moment of happiness.
The evening, the gentle wind stirring the thick branches of
the *tilleul*, the wave of sensuality in him, all of that transformed Julien Sorel into a Rousseauistic dreamer.

On the night that he had his first sexual experience with
Mme. de Rênal he was not happy. He was at that time playing the role of Julien Sorel the peasant conqueror. But after
that experience, when he forgot his predetermined role, he
relaxed into a youthful happiness of love and sensuality.
Happiness with Mme. de Rênal was realized quickly and
easily. But with Mathilde de la Mole, happiness was more
difficult to reach and impossible to hold for long. In his
relationship with Mathilde, Julien suffered as a lover to
such a degree that he often forgot his ambitions in life and
his humble origins in life. There are moments in the second
part of *Le Rouge et le Noir* reminiscent of Goethe's Wer-

ther and Rousseau's Saint-Preux, and of Stendhal himself, when Julien walks by himself at night in places Mathilde had walked and when he contemplates suicide.

The two conflicting sides of Julien's nature that we follow in the first part of *Le Rouge et le Noir*, the ambitious defier of society and the sensitive lover, are fused in the second part where the exercise of his will power and his need for love are so intertwined that one is interchangeable with the other.

In Mathilde, Julien encountered a temperament that was both feminine and masculine. When Julien was not in her presence Mathilde became the type of a dominant personality, determined to maintain her independence. In the Strasbourg episode, Julien became literally the soldier, but all his energies were focused on ways by which to bring Mathilde to terms, to subjugate her by pretending indifference and by camouflaging his love for her.

In his efforts to court the Maréchale de Fervacques (on the advice of Prince Korasoff) and thereby recover Mathilde's love by arousing jealousy in her, he realized that he could, through the support and the intervention of this pious woman influential in the ecclesiastical world, reach a high rank in the Church. But at the same time he had to acknowledge to himself that such an ambition no longer had any meaning for him. Happiness with Mathilde was his one goal. The seeming contradictions of his nature are now harmonized and unified.

The theme of duality, the contrast between a fiery heart of ambition and a loving heart in search of sympathetic affection, returns on the last pages of *Le Rouge et le Noir* and recapitulates the opening of the novel. During his last days in prison Julien gave no evidence of fearing death. He was detached from fear, abstracted, in a sense, from life; and he was able to express in an unusually pure way his opinion of the world and his love for woman. He experienced the two drives of his nature more significantly than he ever had or than he ever would if he were to continue living. The imminence of death permitted him an extraordinary clarification.

First he discussed with himself the justification of his revolt and reached the conclusion that there was no such thing as human rights and no such thing as human morality in an absolute sense. Those men whom he had seen honored in life and living in enviable positions were simply those who had not been caught while committing the crimes that helped to elevate them. The word "virtue" had lost all supernatural and spiritual connotations. It signified that power that permitted man to mount over the heads of other men and gain a vantage point in the sport of society. To succeed is equivalent to becoming the enemy of man. In his final thoughts about man's fate in general and about his own fate in particular, Julien Sorel restated the thoughts we read in the opening scene in his father's sawmill and in the first scenes in the house of M. de Rênal. They constitute the convictions of an anarchist who, because of the corruption of civilization, will not consider as sinful any attack he launches against society. Evil is everywhere and has to be fought by evil.

In the last moments Julien spent with Louise de Rênal in his cell, both of them were able momentarily to transcend the imminence of their separation and enjoy a lightness of spirit, a tone almost of banter and detachment. They were as two children in love who simply in the close presence of one another were able to forget or suppress the sense of doom, the sense of reality. Julien knew deeply in those final moments that happiness is totally simple, that it is made up of a feeling of confidence in the beloved, a feeling of tender-

ness for her, a willingness to give himself over to her—
literally to abandon himself to the ever-present protection of
woman. It was the first maternal role of woman he had
known in life and could hardly remember, and it was the
final role he experienced fleetingly but persuasively in
prison.

Out of the final pages in *Le Rouge et le Noir*, out of the
final moments in the life of Julien Sorel, Stendhal composed
a brief essay on happiness. But the essay is in the form of the
thoughts of Julien and they are totally integrated within the
narration of the novel. The prison cell is converted into the
private room of two lovers where nothing else matters save
the deep affection that one feels for the other. Time has no
meaning save for the present moment that is being lived.
Julien, during that moment, savors an almost mystical form
of happiness.

The resemblance of Julien's attitude toward happiness in
the final scene to the attitude of Fabrice and the other heroes
of Stendhal and to Stendhal's own attitude is a major clue
not only to a fictional hero but to a philosophy of life. The
youthful hero of Stendhal is inevitably changed and re-
created when he lives in an atmosphere of happiness. Stendhal's lesson on happiness stops here, because we never
learn what such a hero would become in later years. . . .
Julien does not kill himself. He dies for what he considers
the absence in the world of the natural rights of man and
the reality of happiness. Such a man's search for happiness
—and this is perhaps Stendhal's most moving message—is
destined to uncover terrifying demonstrations of evil in
human nature.

Julien Sorel is an hallucinatory character. He is a very
specifically characterized individual, and he is also a representative figure of an historical period. He hesitates between

wearing the red cape of a soldier and the black cassock of a priest. By moving from one class to another, he is struck down mortally. In the monstrous strides and the monstrous ambitions of this hero there is a very sensitive young man —weak, loving and full of fear—who incarnates the drama of *le beylisme*.

VI

Lucien Leuwen

DURING HIS SERVICE AS CONSUL in Città Vecchia, Stendhal began in 1834 the writing of a novel he was never to complete, which by critics today is placed very high among his accomplishments, in close company with *Le Rouge et le Noir* and *La Chartreuse de Parme*. It was first known as *Le Chasseur Vert,* the name of a forest inn near Nancy, which corresponds to an episode in the first part of the novel. Stendhal also considered using *L'Oranger de Malte,* and two color titles: *L'amaranthe et le noir* and *Le rouge et le blanc.* He finally chose *Lucien Leuwen,* the name of the book's hero.

The sources of this work are less well known than those of the other novels. But the initial start came from the manuscript of a novel, *Le Lieutenant,* by Stendhal's close friend Mme. Gaulthier, a manuscript she sent to him for criticism in 1833. In his detailed answer to her he listed admonitions and advice very much in keeping with his personal creed of a writer. Delete, he wrote to her, at least fifty superlatives in each chapter. Never say a "burning passion" —it is up to the skill of the writer to make his reader feel the intensity of the passion. When you describe a man or a woman or a landscape, have someone or some place in mind.

From the manuscript of *Le Lieutenant*, which has been lost, Stendhal planned and wrote, in the course of two hundred days, the first three parts of his novel. The fourth part, whose action was destined to take place in Rome, was never written. Part I, as outlined by Stendhal himself, is a picture of French provincial life among the wealthy class. Part II is a passionate love affair and a quarrel. Part III is Parisian life as seen in the world of high finance and politics.

In terms of its political background, *Lucien Leuwen* continues *Le Rouge et le Noir* because Stendhal proposes the analysis of the collapse of the Restoration and the emergence of the newer political form called *Le Juste Milieu*. It is no longer the triumph of the red (Empire) and the black (Restoration), but the triumph of the gray, the reign of Louis-Philippe.

Louis-Philippe was the king of the French, but specifically the king of the moderate and lukewarm citizens. He was the pacifist king. Military life offered in his day no risks, no challenge. Politics was a cautious, insipid career. The army was used only against riots. Only the police force seemed energetic.

Lucien Leuwen, the typically sensitive Stendhal hero, is, thanks almost to chance, *sous-lieutenant* (second lieutenant) in the barracks of Nancy. As he listens to the amorous conquests of his comrades, he worries that he has no capacity for love. Then one day by chance, he meets a simple straightforward young woman who seems worthy of being loved, and he realizes that after all he does have a heart.

Lucien feels disgust for all political intrigue. By the

nobility of his thought and his aspirations, he seems destined for failure in such an age as that of Louis-Philippe. And that is why he turns ultimately to a search for personal happiness. He falls deeply in love, but, in typical Stendhal fashion, he will be harassed by a stupid intrigue. Stendhal and Balzac both had a strong predilection for the melodramatic, for the banal scandal of a *fait divers*. When the woman Lucien loves, Mme. de Chasteller, gives birth secretly to a baby she must have conceived before she knew him, he is overcome with disappointment and despair.

M. Leuwen, Lucien's father, is one of the great characters of the book. He would most certainly be, from Stendhal's viewpoint, the ideal father. He is one of the directors of the banking firm Van Peters, Leuwen and Company. A man who fears two things: boredom and humidity in the atmosphere. He never appears serious or reprimanding toward his son. At one moment in a conversation, when Lucien acknowledges all he owes his father and his shame of not having returned any of the paternal generosity, M. Leuwen accuses him of becoming a *saint-simonien* and warns him that he would thus become tiresome. *Est-ce que tu deviendrais saint-simonien par hasard? Comme tu vas être ennuyeux!* He sends his son off to entertain some ballet dancers of the Opéra. The tone of banter and wit that the father takes with his son is always in good taste and always pointedly helpful. The authority he exercises is always expressed with an indulgent smile and a very subtly articulated commiseration. He maintains in his role of father the litheness and the affected indifference of a young man. Lucien himself is far more dramatically constituted. Although he feels a son's respect for his father, it often takes second place to the outbursts of his heart, to expressions of horror over his predicaments.

In the long conversation between father and son, where the feelings of the two men, one sixty-five and the other twenty-four, are alternately expressed and concealed, the entire novel is recast and recapitulated. Lucien's thoughts are neither on the army nor on marriage nor on the career of a banker. M. Leuwen points out that for four years there has been no reason for shedding blood in France. If Lucien is considering entering politics, the father wonders whether the boy is enough of a scoundrel to assume such a post.

Lucien consents to meet the minister and is amazed when his father keeps the minister waiting. M. Leuwen explains that the minister needs the Leuwen bank and is afraid of the Leuwen salon. The entire Chapter 46 is a masterpiece that opens with a portrait of Lucien's father. This celebrated banker spends his time with witty diplomats rather than with the solemn ones, and with dancers from the Opéra. On the whole, he is bored by "correct" society, *la bonne société*. He changes his clothes five or six times a day, depending on how much wind is blowing. His conversation abounds in wit and tends toward indiscretion. Elevated thoughts are not his concern. He speaks his complete thoughts, the truth as he sees it on any subject, only to his wife who worships him. She is his second memory, and he trusts her more than he trusts his own memory. Gradually, in the presence of his son (his wife enjoys having Lucien with them), he begins expressing his complete thoughts, about whatever is being discussed. He trusts Lucien's discretion. The clue to M. Leuwen is his lightness of heart and gaiety.

The conversation between father and son reveals not only their points of opposition, but especially the multiple almost secret ways in which they are close to one another. The emotion that might have been expressed between the older and the younger man is always being disguised by irony. With the exceptions of his wife and son, M. Leuwen scorns all of mankind, those in high positions and those in very lowly positions.

At the death of his father, there is no fortune left, and Lucien takes the position of second secretary in an embassy in Capel. He will return to Paris only after his financial ruin has been forgotten. He stopped for two days at Lake Geneva and visited the places made famous by Rousseau's *La Nou-velle Héloïse*. There he indulged in a moment of sadness and nostalgia. He was sentimentally moved by his visits to Milan, Pavia, Bologna, Florence. Before reaching his post in Capel, he had to discipline himself in order to develop an attitude of coolness and detachment toward people.

In many ways, *Lucien Leuwen* is Stendhal's novel of his consulship in Cività Vecchia. The leading traits of M. Leu-wen, his sensitivity to the cold, his general boredom with life, his scorn for honors and for most members of the human race, are all characteristics of Stendhal himself. Lucien, in his suffering over love, and in his failure to find happiness in a world that fundamentally disgusts him, completes the picture of Stendhal. But the youthful protagonist seems to take second place to the father.

Despite the marked difference of class, Lucien tempera-mentally and psychologically is closer to Julien Sorel than to other Stendhal heroes. One senses from the very start that under the serene and smiling and polished exterior there is a tension of spirit and a capacity for exaltation that are will-fully concealed in Lucien. From the beginning of his life, Lucien knows the laws of society that Julien will come to know very fast, and they both sense how ludicrous, how futile any demonstration of heroics would appear in Paris society. Such a society forces Julien to be a hypocrite and forces Lucien to be an epicurean, even if hypocrisy and epicureanism are contrary to their natures. All the natural instincts of their temperament have to be altered and disciplined and redirected.

In his own way, and almost as deliberately and fearlessly as a boy of the lower class, Lucien Leuwen has to learn how to adapt himself to society and cultivate in himself manners and behavior that will disguise the beautiful spontaneity of his nature. Lucien and Julien accept the necessity, in such a society as theirs, of seeking honors and thereby humiliating themselves. Even if such humiliations are brief and tentative, they represent a turning away from bravery, from the exaltation of one man's power that Stendhal once called *espagnolisme*. These heroes' basic drive toward nobility and greatness in achievement is contradicted. They are forced to play the role of clowns at court. Their revolt has to remain hidden. What they learn best in such behavior is self-discipline.

In his electoral campaign in Normandy, Lucien learns how to deal with men in order to use them. He calculates and plans with as much astuteness as Julien Sorel does in the Hôtel de la Mole. In their initiations to love, which are comparable to battle skirmishes, they learn how to curb their instincts and their spontaneity. There is no sense of abandonment or total giving over to the experience of love. Their attitude toward it is as forced as their social politeness. There is no crisis in Lucien's life story comparable to Julien's when he shoots Mme. de Rênal in church and thereby yields to his natural instincts, but there is a similar pattern of development of a planned campaign to combat life and society that ends with a possible release of instinctive, disinterested and noble feelings. After his training, largely conducted by his father, to take on a complex society and succeed within it, Lucien is able, at least momentarily, to enjoy relaxation at Lake Geneva and an indulgence in sentiments. The sensibility of a Stendhal hero is allowed to express itself directly only after it has been disciplined and silenced by unfavorable social circumstances.

The theme of three of Stendhal's novels, which form a kind of triptych, is the hero's difficult confrontation with society, so difficult, in fact, that he appears as an outsider, as one doomed not to succeed. Each of the three heroes comes from a different social class: Julien Sorel, in *Le Rouge et le Noir,* from the peasant or lower class; Lucien Leuwen, from the higher bourgeoisie; and Fabrice del Dongo, in *La Chartreuse de Parme,* from the aristocracy. The conflict between the hero and society is not central in *Armance,* where Octave de Malivert has to adjust to a physical defect rather than to a social-political world.

All four of these heroes, and especially Lucien, tend to live in a dreamworld where they are never fully aware of their advantages, especially of the advantages of their good looks and the purely physical charm of their personalities. But of course, part of their charm comes precisely from this lack of awareness of how they affect people. Stendhal, who is in them all, stops their story always at that point when they would normally pass beyond their dreamworld and when their physical appearance would change from youthfulness to maturity. In each case, Stendhal, the writer and the consul, survives in order to tell the story of his own youth or rather the story of his idealized youth.

When Lucien is expelled from the Ecole Polytechnique, probably because of his republican leanings, his father secures for him a commission as second lieutenant in the Twenty-seventh Lancers, a regiment garrisoned in Nancy. There Lucien finds the same political divisions that existed in Paris: the moderates or those belonging to the *juste milieu*, who support Louis-Philippe; the ultras, who hope for the return from exile of Charles X; and the republicans. He feels that he is an outsider. Stendhal uses the same word that Albert Camus will make famous one hundred years later: *je resterai un étranger parmi eux*.

Stendhal provides in *Lucien Leuwen* a very detailed and at times merciless picture of the French political situation in 1832. Between politics and love, he develops a subtle but important relationship. In a life given over to the machinations of politics, to the lies and hypocrisies of partisanship, the sentimental side of man's nature is atrophied. Love is seen as the saving power of man's nature, the force that will protect him against the deficiencies and maliciousness and disintegrating forces of his age.

The pattern of the hero attracted to two women very different in temperament, which is in *Le Rouge et le Noir* (Julien attracted to Louise de Rênal and Mathilde) and in *La Chartreuse de Parme* (Fabrice attracted to Gina and Clélia), is also in *Lucien Leuwen* where the hero carries on a flirtation with the complacent Mme. d'Hocquincourt and feels a deep love for Mme. Bathilde de Chasteller. Lucien leaves Nancy when he is led to believe that Mme. de Chasteller has had a child by another man. This is the abrupt ending of the first volume. In Paris, in the second volume, the political scene is described in great detail. Lucien becomes an assistant to the minister of the interior (*le Maître des Requêtes*) but he is still in love with Bathilde. Although Lucien serves his political masters, he is not contaminated by the evil of politics. He remains inwardly the innocent.

M. Leuwen occupies much of the last part of the book. When he tries to form an opposition party, it is presented as a political maneuvering both comical and subversive.

The comic stratagem, annunciatory of Proust's sense of comedy, is apparent in the scene where M. Leuwen tells Mme. Grandet that her husband will have the government position he wants, provided that she become the mistress of his son Lucien!

In the salons of Nancy and Paris, the cultivated politeness of manner in Lucien masks his natural character, the spontaneous naturalness of his character. If he had appeared outside of his particular social world, he would have resembled a tragic hero, a courageous young man unified in his instincts and destined to catastrophe. He conceals his exaltation as he tries to eradicate from his behavior all expansiveness and forcefulness, all trace of *espagnolisme*. Unlike the romantic heroes, he does not indulge in narcissism. His heroism is his adaptation to the social comedy that is being played around him. This adaptation is in direct contradiction with what he wants to ask of society and of the world: a heroic life of adventure. As he listened to the lancers talk in the barracks of Nancy, he imagined great deeds to perform and magnificent perils to face: *il ne voyait que de grandes choses à faire et de beaux périls* (Book I, Chapter 17). Lucien is the typical Stendhal hero in the sense that he imagines an existence that would have the purity and nobility of a classical tragedy, and yet he is forced to live within a social comedy of triteness and meanness and bathos. His father understands this conflict in Lucien, and he explains it lucidly when he points out to his son that the boy imagines men as being greater than they are and too often converts the men who speak to him into heroes. How can a boy's natural instincts toward greatness be allowed to grow in a world that has lost the propensity, the setting, the dimension of tragedy and has become a small society based on platitudes and hypocrisies?

Of all Stendhal's heroes, Lucien is the most influenced by the society from which he wants to escape. His vanity has been nurtured by the Paris salons, and it is harder for him than for the others to recover the spontaneity and the naturalness of his temperament. In Nancy, he tries to overcome his vanity and to move beyond the lessons of his father and Paris society. Lucien is preoccupied with his conscience, with the moral dictates of his conscience, and in this he differs from Julien Sorel whose morality is one of action.

Lucien knows that he has been favored by his birth and by the advantages of his social position. His problem is quite simply how will he be able to live in his kind of world and esteem himself. He will not have any self-esteem if he is satisfied with what the world offers him. The favors from life that come to Lucien are treated by him as obstacles to the peace of his conscience. This is the moral center of the book. The novel is the story of a young man's sense of morality, and yet whenever M. Leuwen *père* is present the interest shifts to him, and the principal theme of the novel is overshadowed. M. Leuwen is success itself—financial and worldly—and he possesses a nature not at all preoccupied with the problem of self-esteem which we find in Lucien. He has self-esteem, and there is no problem. In the presence of M. Leuwen, Lucien becomes the son and ceases being the protagonist. This would seem to be a defect in the book's construction that might have been changed had the novel been completed.

VII

The Personal Writings

IN HIS ART AS NOVELIST, Stendhal never uses directly the activities and adventures of his own life and never draws directly upon his personal suffering. The tone of self-complacency and the habit of the unabashed self-confession of the typical romantic writer are totally absent in Stendhal's novels. By means of the style and the plots of his books, he created a distance between himself and his readers. If in a fundamentally psychic sense he identifies himself with his heroes; his heroes are not recognizably Stendhal in any exterior sense. He separated his personal writings from his novels. His autobiography is to be found in two books: *Souvenirs d'égotisme* of 1832 and *Vie de Henry Brulard* of 1836.

The first of these writings, the *Souvenirs*, is a scrupulous self-analysis. With no desire to idealize his features or exalt his traits, Stendhal quite resolutely wrote about himself for the purpose of reaching some degree of self-knowledge. He had just begun his consulate service in Cività Vecchia and had considerable leisure ahead of him, when he announced his intention of using this leisure (*pour employer mes loisirs*) in that foreign land for the purpose of writing out what happened to him during his Paris years of 1821 to 1830. Did he do all within his power to reach happiness at the time of the minor and major events in his life during those nine years? What kind of man had he become? What was the quality of his mind? His self-evaluation had varied so much from day to day, from month to month, that he now distrusted his judgments. He was struck by the fact that his judgments had varied as much as his disposition had fluctuated. . . . With these opening questions, Stendhal announced the frankness with which he hoped to write about himself and the rigorous tone reminiscent of a La Rochefoucauld with which he planned to consign his observations to paper.

This tone of honesty and scrupulosity with respect to difficult personal problems we have come to associate with the personal journal of the twentieth century, with André Gide, for example, and Julien Green. There is no reason to believe that Stendhal ever planned to publish his *Souvenirs d'égotisme*, but he did plan to leave it with his papers for the use of posterity.

The word *égotisme*, as used by Stendhal, has often been given a Nietzschean-like meaning, equivalent to a superman's drive to reach happiness at any cost. The worship of oneself, the cult of self-development, is a concept not applicable to Stendhal. The cult of the self, as found in such a romantic work as Musset's *Confession d'un enfant du siècle* and much later in the writings of Maurice Barrès, is not what Stendhal meant by egotism. Stendhal exhibits an interest in himself because of a greater interest in analysis itself, because of his belief that analysis is a therapeutic exercise by means of which a man's disposition can be understood and improved. Stendhal is not self-admiring, as Rousseau is, in his *Confessions*. He is not presenting himself as an exceptional human being whose sensitivity sets him apart from mankind, in the manner Chateaubriand develops in his autobiography *Mémoires d'outre-tombe*.

The two texts *Egotisme* and *Henry Brulard* are self-appraisals which have the value of documents, first, and of a literary art, second. As he wrote them, he had probably very little sense of the value they were to possess today, and yet they are the texts in which Stendhal's mind is the sharpest, in which his powers of observation are the most developed. In these two books, as well as in his letters and other personal writings, Stendhal appears the moralist, in the manner of a Montaigne and a Gide—a man inhabiting a moral world, who is determined to analyze his conduct in that world in terms of the prevalent moral conventions and in terms of the hypocrisy by which moral conventions are sustained. We see Stendhal play a social role and participate in the game of society, and at the same time we see him trying to preserve in himself and express his most spontaneous feelings and his noblest impulses. There is peril, obviously, in these two ways of behavior, both moral and social peril. Precisely these forms of peril are the substance of *Souvenirs d'égotisme* and *Vie de Henry Brulard*. Henri Beyle is the lonely hero of these two books, and he is actually far more lonely than his lonely heroes, Julien Sorel and Octave and Fabrice del Dongo.

The situation in which Beyle found himself in Cività Vecchia was similar to the Renaissance poet Du Bellay's situation in Rome which stimulated the writing of his sonnets *Les Regrets*. Beyle nostalgically recalled the Paris he had known and his Parisian friends, as Du Bellay in his exile had recalled the simplicity of his native Anjou. A basic modesty in speaking about himself, in revealing secrets about himself probably kept Stendhal from writing more than he did in *Souvenirs d'égotisme*. His determination to be honest vied with his instinct to conceal his more intimate thoughts.

Vie de Henry Brulard is the story of his life through adolescence. It is the third of Stendhal's books to rally an impressive number of admirers who are anxious to announce the outstanding book: Is it *Le Rouge et le Noir* or *La Chartreuse de Parme* or *Vie de Henry Brulard?* Those who give first place to *Vie de Henry Brulard* base their claims on the boldness with which Stendhal explored his past and sought to recover time that had been lost. About to turn fifty (*je vais avoir cinquante ans*), Stendhal declared it was time to know himself, or to know the boy and the man he was. What was to count the most for him was simplicity and honesty in the narration. The determination to speak the truth explains why he took pen in hand. He will go back much farther in time than the nine years he recalls in *Souvenirs d'égotisme*, and the effort to recall and record will be much more painful. In late November 1835, in San Pietro, as he watched the panorama of Rome spread out before him in the sunlight, he decided to write his autobiography. He worked on it until March 1836, and by that time he had reached in his life story his first visit to Milan. At that point, he interrupted the work and never completed it.

The pseudonym Brulard is not easy to explain. It may have come from the name of a notary, a first cousin of Dr. Gagnon, on his mother's side of the family. He never rewrote or reworked any of the passages in the manuscript because of his belief that the first draft of such writing would be the most accurate, the most truthful. The portraits he gives of his childhood and adolescence are precious commentaries for an understanding of his work. The genesis and the development of his sensibility and his thought are carefully described and annotated.

Stendhal succeeds in resurrecting moments of his past and giving them a freshness as if they had been lived the day before he wrote, rather than thirty-five or forty years earlier. The facts of chronological time do not count as much as the power of the writer's memory which is able, on the most striking pages of *Vie de Henry Brulard* to reinstate the past within the present. . . .

Such a meticulous scholar as Paul Arbalet who has written extensively on the early years of Stendhal's life (*La Jeunesse de Stendhal*) has discovered errors in facts and dates in *Vie de Henry Brulard,* and he has proved quite conclusively that the portraits of the father, Chérubin Beyle and the priest Abbé Raillane, represented them as more sinister than they actually were. But such points, made in the name of historical truth, do not alter the veracity Stendhal records of the effect of such figures on the young boy Henri Beyle. The writer is concerned with relating the truthfulness of his reactions to people and events and to the city of Grenoble.

He yearned for affection and did not receive it. When, in the country setting of Les Echelles, he experienced happiness by simply being in close proximity to young women in beautiful dresses, the transport he felt was of such a nature that it was impossible to analyze. In narrating his life, Stendhal moves back and forth between sentiments of suspicion and despair, and sentiments of elation and daydreaming. The man is already in the child. The entire book is an explicit document on the explanation and the analysis of a temperament that was fully formed at a very early age. The memory of a sensation leads him to a very concrete scene he is able to recall. He trusts the sensation. He distrusts the judgments of others and his own judgments. Scrupulously he moves into his past and tries not to alter or embroider his memories. What happened to Henri Beyle we see happening at the moment when we are reading the text.

Souvenirs d'égotisme begins, in 1832, with the end of Stendhal's great love for Métilde Dembowska. But he is too close to that suffering to write about it. Throughout the book there are a large number of portraits. The meditations about himself are grouped especially at the beginning. The rest of the work is concerned with episodes and anecdotes.

The portraits undoubtedly suffer from a lack of rewriting. Those portraits that seem the best are based on models from whom Stendhal was the most detached emotionally. The proprietor of the Hôtel de Bruxelles, M. Petit, is a good example of a portrait Stendhal struck off that is successful because of an absence of any emotional involvement. Mérimée is clearly described in certain salon scenes, but the reason for his friendship with Beyle is not clear. Destutt de Tracy is given a fuller portrait, especially in his physical appearance and in the casualness of his conversation. Métilde Dembowska and her cousin Madame Traversi are only vaguely sketched.

The personal meditations, of which there are many, follow a similar pattern. They start up because of a need to write, and they proceed without plan, without organization. The themes are repetitive. The questions asked by the writer are numerous, but the answers given are few. The kind of writing, so obviously improvised in *Souvenirs*, does not permit Stendhal to judge himself, to judge the events of his past and to measure their importance. He oscillates too much from theme to theme, and without the necessary details, to reach any conclusions about the relative importance of events and thoughts.

Stendhal is more intriguing, more successful, in the purely narrative sections of *Souvenirs d'égotisme*. For the story of an event, he chooses details that are both important and vivid. These parts of the work do not need rewriting. His remarkable memory serves him well, as well as his power of imagination and his ability to imagine the circumstances of the scenes. Whenever his heart is involved, as with the appearance of Countess Curial in his life, he avoids any real analysis. This kind of commentary is reserved for the novels. The writing of *Souvenirs* was interrupted by Stendhal's activities in Cività Vecchia, but even if he had continued, he would probably not have written any real analyses of his loves and of his temptations to love. That part of his life remained within his memory, to be recast in his novels. The telling portraits he is able to write out so swiftly, the dream or meditation sequences and the constant check he makes on his mental attitudes—all of this is announced in *Souvenirs d'égotisme* and will be pursued in the writing of *Vie de Henry Brulard*.

Stendhal had no intention of making *Vie de Henry Brulard* correspond to a given technique of writing, or even, for that matter, to a given genre. The book is both an effort to recall the past and a struggle, as the sentences are being consigned to paper, to be sincere and truthful. Whenever he digresses from the narrative, he indulges in that kind of meditation and revery for which he has a marked predilection: *Je vois que la rêverie a été ce que j'ai préféré à tout, même à passer pour homme d'esprit.* In recomposing his memories, Stendhal tends to alter the accuracy of facts in order to write a story that will appear logical and likely.

It is paradoxical that the writer's sincerity in both Rousseau and Stendhal tended to deform accuracy. The tone of sincerity is reached at the expense of historical truth.

On turning fifty, Stendhal seems suddenly aware that most of his life is behind him. The past is a treasure house, out of which he can call up the memory of his loves and try to pass judgment on them. As he writes, the past comes back and he ceases worrying about whether he will forget essential episodes. The scenes are fragments from a life rather than a continuous narrative of a childhood. Their power comes from the imperious sense of truthfulness with which Stendhal endows them (even if factual accuracy is sometimes sacrificed). A close reader seldom has the impression that such and such an episode is invented. Stendhal convinces us of his veracity, to such a degree that we recognize the bareness and the cruelty of certain childhood experiences.

What is Stendhal's method of writing in the *Vie de Henry Brulard?* He says that by writing about an event, he sees it more clearly. His childhood memories, as memories in his mind, are amorphous and covered over by a strange light whose source seems to be the acuteness of the original sensations that accompanied the experiences. In writing of them he instinctively employs a scientific method by which he will see friends and members of his family and other acquaintances as *genres*. He tends to classify human beings as a botanist classifies plants. His mind still holds the pictures of the physical traits of these characters thirty or forty years later, but he begins to understand the traits only when he begins writing about them. Some of the characters whom he observed as a child have disappeared from his memory. The fresco of his past is incomplete.

Stendhal's method is a mental investigation of the past. An image comes to his mind and he begins describing it, and thereupon many details rush into his mind and he realizes he understands and sees the past thanks to this exercise of writing it down. As the writing of a given scene continues everything comes to life: furniture in a room, the design of the room, human features, gestures and activities. They are scenes that have been preserved in his memory because of some deeply felt emotion: anger, for example, or sorrow. When his emotion returns clear to him, he is then able to analyze it and to understand it more fully than he had when it was originally experienced. Stendhal is very much bent on exploring the significance of a given scene. The intensity of the emotion that accompanied the scene is a clue and guide for this research. Within the scenes where Stendhal is describing members of his family, the sense of an autobiography gives way to the sense of a novel, as Henry Brulard takes on the proportions of a protagonist.

The first two chapters are the prelude to *Vie*, at the end of which Stendhal announces that he is going to be born: *je vais naître*. Then, in the third chapter, he strikes off in rapid succession vignettes of four members of his family, and one senses immediately the importance of these characters in the formative years of his life and the place they occupy in his memory.

The opening portrait, the briefest of all, may well be, in the psychoanalytical sense, the profoundest, the most traumatic of the four. It is clearly significant that he opens with his earliest memory, that of his cousin Mme. Pison du Galland, a young woman twenty-five years old, slightly overweight, who used considerable rouge. The dominance of the rouge seems to have irritated the very young boy. It is a pastoral scene, in a field of daisies. He had refused to kiss his cousin. She insisted and so he bit her on the cheek or the forehead. The opening line narrates this act of violence:

Mon premier souvenir est d'avoir mordu à la joue ou au front Madame Pison du Galland, ma cousine . . . and then, Stendhal describes the background of the incident.

He passes immediately to the second portrait which is related to the first. His aunt Séraphie seized on this episode of the bite to call the boy a monster and to point out to the family his disreputable disposition. It is her disposition, rather, that comes to light. Séraphie is described as a pious old maid about whose past Stendhal knows almost nothing. It is enough that she became the boy's enemy from the beginning of his life. On the balcony of the second floor of the house on Grande Rue in Grenoble, young Henri had made a garden and from there one day, he dropped a knife into the street below. It dropped close to a Madame Chenevaz, and Séraphie instantly deduces that Henri had planned an assassination. For the second time, Séraphie uses the adjective *atroce* to characterize Henri. She was his tormentor during his entire childhood. He implies that she became his father's mistress after his mother's death. On their walks together, he was often the third unwelcomed party. This belief that Séraphie has replaced his mother largely accounted for his break with his father.

Henri's first revolt against Séraphie took place when he was four. Because of his aunt's piety, the boy rejected religion at that age. He felt a horror for religious practice, a sentiment that it took him several years to temper and bring down to some more reasonable proportions. His first hero, a man of liberal enlightened ideas, was his grandfather, Henri Gagnon. This man was devoted to Voltaire and had once gone on a pilgrimage to Ferney to see Voltaire in person. In this third portrait of Chapter 3, Stendhal speaks of the honor he felt as a child when he was allowed to touch the bust of Voltaire in his grandfather's study and office, but he also points out how little the great writer was to count for him in the years ahead. Henri Gagnon was a distinguished physician. His powdered wig, with its three rows of curls, his small hat he carried in his hand but never wore are described, and his two passions he bequeathed to his grandson: Hippocrates (a text he read in Latin although he knew Greek) and Horace.

The fourth portrait in the early chapter, and one that has been fully exploited by Stendhal biographers, is that of his mother Henriette Gagnon, whom he refers to, significantly, as Henriette. She died when the boy was seven. He was in love with her: *j'étais amoureux de ma mère*. The sexual traits of this love are quite specifically listed in one short passage in which Stendhal expresses the desire he had felt as a young boy to cover his mother with kisses when she was nude. *Je voulais couvrir ma mère de baisers et qu'il n'y eût pas de vêtements*. Stendhal records that Henriette loved her son passionately and was constantly kissing him. When he returned the kisses, she was often forced to leave his presence. At his mother's death, he was so grieved that he was unable to cry in a normal fashion, and Séraphie reproached him for not loving his mother! Henri Beyle's moral life began, as he claims, with his intense love for his mother. This love was the immediate cause of his hate for his father. Son and father were opposites temperamentally. This hate was doubtless the strongest element in Beyle's antipathy toward Grenoble society and in fact toward all of society.

In the fifth chapter the portrait of Henri's young uncle, Romain Gagnon, son of the grandfather Henri Gagnon, offers a relief in the sombre picture of the family. The young lawyer is described by Stendhal as one of the most pleasant people of Grenoble who took the lad Henri to a performance of *Le Cid* where the actor playing Rodrigue almost put his eyes out through a bungling gesture with his sword as he recited the *stances* at the end of Act I. Henri enjoyed some degree of intimacy with his uncle who allowed the lad to watch him change, at the end of the day, from his formal office clothes to a dressing gown (*robe de chambre*) before supper in the late evening. The special privilege that delighted young Henri was to carry a silver candlestick and precede his Uncle Romain on the way down from the third floor of the house on the Place Grenette to the second floor.

Henri Beyle was puzzled by the grandfather's seeming dislike for his son. The young lawyer evidently was not sufficiently well read to satisfy such a cultivated man as Henri Gagnon. He provided his son with room and board during the years before his marriage. The boy believed his Uncle Romain received gifts of money from wealthy mistresses and thus was able to dress in elegant fashion and at the same time support poorer mistresses!

Stendhal reminds his readers that such customs in Grenoble are related in *Les Liaisons Dangereuses* of Choderlos de Laclos. At the time of Henriette Beyle's death in 1790, Romain Gagnon was twenty-five. He married and settled down in Les Echelles in Savoie a few years later. From that time on, he returned to Grenoble intermittently to see his former mistresses. The boy's visits to Les Echelles gave him great pleasure and the pleasure was associated with his warm feelings for his uncle. Those visits helped efface from his thoughts Séraphie and his father and the desolate Grenoble house of the rue des Vieux Jésuites. In his often repeated efforts to establish a relationship with Italy, Stendhal refers to the Roman head of his Uncle Romain (Chapter 38). The young lawyer's success with women impressed the boy and later when he comments on this success in *Henry Brulard*, he inevitably associates this sexual achievement with the classic story of Grenoble, *Les Liaisons Dangereuses* (Chapter 39).

When he was a very young boy, his mother represented for him an object of sensual desire, and during the years after her death, young Romain Gagnon was a model of success in love-making and the object of admiration for the boy. This sensual preoccupation with woman never diminished in Beyle's life, and even during his boyhood, it threw every other kind of adventure or activity into a secondary position or even into disrepute. By contrast with the early sensuality of his nature, his other feelings were usually sharpened into a form of disgust or disapproval.

His father Joseph-Chérubin Beyle, whose character is analyzed at some length in Chapter 7, was the object of such dislike that it is difficult to account for it except as a strong reaction to the sensual attraction and the hero worship the boy felt for Henriette and Romain. Henri Beyle ascribed to his father, in a long list of complaints, such traits as avariciousness and an excessive love for money, an inveterate dislike for literature and philosophy, and a false interest in his son, based not on affection but on the belief that the boy would continue the family line. He blames his father for the total lack of happiness in his childhood. He pursued the study of mathematics largely because he saw in it a means of escaping from Grenoble, which he loathed for many reasons most of which were associated with his father. In one sentence of extreme violence, he accuses his Aunt Séraphie and his father of being two devils bent upon converting him into a slave.

Stendhal wrote in some detail about his father's passion for agriculture and the *domaine* he owned in Claix outside of Grenoble at a distance of two leagues. His cultivation of this land is interpreted as an example of shrewdness and love of financial profit. His father had the habit of walking on foot between Grenoble and Claix, and this exercise, according to his son, strengthened his body and prolonged his life. Chérubin Beyle spoke endlessly of his *domaine* to Henri as if it were for him a status symbol. On their walks together in the fields, the son had to listen to the calculations and the profits that the future would bring about from such an investment. A forty-volume set of Voltaire's works was kept at Claix. The boy would steal one volume at a time to look at the engravings. He found these engravings ridiculous and indicates that already at that age he had developed a taste in art that would allow him one day to write such a work as the *Histoire de la peinture en Italie.*

Henriette Beyle's death created a change in the family life. Chérubin Beyle put a small bed for Henri in the alcove of his room, did away with servants in his house and took his meals in the house of the boy's grandfather. He broke off all social relationships in the city of Grenoble.

The first Latin tutor of the boy was a M. Joubert, a type of pedant and an ineffectual teacher. His successor, Abbé Raillane, is presented in *Vie de Henry Brulard* (Chapter 7) as a scoundrel devoid of any human feelings. This Provençal priest, who was incapable of clear thinking and reasoning, had been hired by Chérubin Beyle through a sense of vanity. To have attached to his household a Latin preceptor for his son would be a striking social advantage in the city. Stendhal's memories of Abbé Raillane are associated with ugliness and filth. The priest raised canaries in a large cage, about thirty at once, and kept the cage close to his pupil's bed. At daybreak the birds would begin a racket that woke the boy up. The smell from the cage was strong, and the room in which the priest and his pupil slept was humid and airless. Abbé Raillane represented to young Henri a form of tyranny he detested, and this regimen turned the boy into a malcontent. His hatred for his father became coupled with his hatred for the priest.

Emotionally Stendhal separated himself from his family, and intellectually he separated himself from the bourgeoisie. But he confessed that he could not have lived with the proletariat. He was a new kind of aristocrat, always out of place socially and intellectually, and that is why he founded, in his mind, a tiny community of the "happy few." What Baudelaire was to call *dandysme* corresponded quite closely to Stendhal's attitude. It was a form of isolation, on many levels: artistic, social, intellectual. *Vie de Henry Brulard* is a lengthy explanation and rationalization of this position. It is the demonstration of how a man's life turned into the enactment of a drama of excessive solitude. He himself became the characters in his life. His abundant use of pseudonyms is a proof of the need he felt to multiply his personality. It is significant that throughout *Henry Brulard*, Henri Beyle never tries to solve the dilemma of his life and of his character. He is quite content with reasoning about it and elucidating it. He learned to live with the drama of the many selves, and in his fiction, always depicted the same situation of the hero unable to fit into whatever society and whatever situation were his.

One of the persistent faults of Stendhal critics has been to make him into a thinker and even a philosopher. He was not that. His mind was trained by wide reading in systematic thinkers, of whom a few, especially Destutt de Tracy and Cabanis, seem to have remained intellectual guides for him throughout his life. But he was far from being a materialist in philosophy. More than his intellectual training Stendhal stresses in *Vie de Henry Brulard* the development of his temperament, his inflammatory and impassioned disposition. This he calls *espagnolisme* and attributes it to the Gagnon family and to their Italian origins.

Paul Arbalet, who has written the most detailed account of Stendhal's background and prevenience, believes that the Gagnons did come from Italy and that the novelist's temperament represented a fusion of a southern form of passion with a Provençal sense of practicality that was strengthened by the eighteenth-century *philosophes*. Critics have tended to use the two terms of *logique* and *espagnolisme* in an effort to explain two aspects of Stendhal's temperament. The complex sensibility of the writer is not easily defined by such precise terms. But of the two overused terms, *espagnolisme* comes closer to Stendhal's nature as revealed in *Henry Brulard*, namely his reactions to all kinds of experience. His reactions are vivid. They are pursued with a veritable obstinacy and are always accompanied by a determined reasonableness in understanding the experience.

The word *sensibilité* is often used in key passages where Stendhal tries to measure the degree of sensibility that affects him under given circumstances. He claims that the vividness of his sensibility has remained steadfast throughout his life but that he has learned how to conceal it, whenever concealment would be appropriate. He learned how to disguise the richness of his feelings by an affectation of irony. His enjoyment of landscapes (*la vue des beaux paysages*) is the reason for his travels. Landscapes play upon his sensibility and have the power of helping him to understand human traits better, especially traits in women he loves. They stimulate his meditations (*rêveries*), which give him more pleasure than anything else in life.

At times, but quite infrequently, the reasonableness of Stendhal's nature (his *logique*) was in conflict with his emotional flamboyance (his *espagnolisme*), but usually one mood is indulged in at a time. This is true also for his leading characters. They appear either calculating and very much in possession of their faculties, or they appear in moments of frenzy and emotional upheaval. The discipline of logic is periodically replaced by the exceptional vitality of an emotion in Henri Beyle or in Julien Sorel.

The analysis of Henry Brulard's love life, and notably of his amorous defeats, involves these two words of *logique*, which would signify his planned strategy of conquest, and *espagnolisme*, which would be the elated feelings of courtship that almost inevitably ended in defeat, in what Stendhal habitually calls *fiasco*, or sexual impotence. Quietly and pathetically he records that most of the women he had loved had resisted him. The most likely hypothesis to explain this pattern of related fiasco is a sexual impotence that might have been brought about by excessive planning for sexual achievement, by a too-constant cerebration about love and love-making. Even if his thoughts were steadily fixed on sex, Stendhal was probably not, in the strict sense, highly sexual. It would seem that when the time for the act came, an inevitable shyness prevailed. Such shyness would quite normally increase with each defeat. . . . However, such a theory as this, by its very nature, has to be hypothetical. The sexual impotence, implied in this theory, would not necessarily be permanent but, rather, intermittent.

In *Lamiel*, the heroine, through a desire to lose her virginity, gives a peasant boy a sum of money to have sexual intercourse with her, and in the novella *L'Abbesse de Castro*, the abbess in question upbraids a bishop after he has taken her sexually. But apart from these episodes, it would be difficult to find any experience in Stendhal's fiction that approaches the pornographic in vocabulary or act. On the other hand, there is at times coarseness of expression in the *Journal* and *Vie de Henry Brulard*. Martin Turnell in *The Novel in France* points out the resemblance, in this regard, between Stendhal and Baudelaire, another *grand timide*.

Although *Henry Brulard* narrates only the first eighteen years of Stendhal's life, the many digressions depict or refer to important days and events in his later life. His precursor in this form of writing and his model, at least to some degree, was unquestionably Jean-Jacques Rousseau. Both *Vie de Henry Brulard* and *Les Confessions* provoke the reader's curiosity and impell him to continue the reading. But Rousseau emphasizes the justification of his acts, and Stendhal emphasizes a search for the reasons that caused him to act in any given way. The novelist's capacity for feeling and for reacting to experiences characterizes his entire life, but it was only a long time after the experience of feeling the effect of words said to him, or landscapes seen by him, or minute events in his relationship with Séraphie, Henriette, Chérubin, Romain, Raillane that he reached any understanding of them. And critics today are exploring a deeper understanding than that recorded in *Vie de Henry Brulard* of some of the meanings in events and experiences in Stendhal's childhood: his biting the cheek of his cousin, his love for his mother, his hatred for his father, the stench from Abbé Raillane's cage of canaries.

VIII

La Chartreuse de Parme

BEFORE WRITING HIS ARTICLE of praise about *La Chartreuse de Parme,* Balzac read the book three times for his pleasure. This fact in itself was a compensation for the very small number of articles that the book, on its appearance, elicited. This novel, more than any other of Stendhal, makes still today demands of attentiveness and patience and sympathy on the part of the reader. It has been called Stendhal's first novel because it seems to be the farthest away from Stendhal's own experience in life and from his private obsessions.

It is quite possible to prefer *Le Rouge et le Noir* to *La Chartreuse de Parme.* It is quite possible to prefer now one and now the other; and this is true for most fervent Stendhal readers. One of the most celebrated of these readers, André Gide, confessed that this was true for him. He claimed that *Le Rouge et le Noir* has a greater impact on the reader, a more dramatic, more surprising impact, but he analyzed the continuous charm that *La Chartreuse de Parme* exerts on its readers. On every reading, *La Chartreuse* becomes a different book: *A chaque fois qu'on y revient, c'est un nouveau livre qu'on lit.*

As in his remarkable pages on *Armance,* Gide goes to the heart of the matter when he discusses what he considers the cardinal virtue of *La Chartreuse,* namely its gratuitousness. *C'est un livre gratuit,* Gide writes, and by this expression, he means to point out the pleasure with which Stendhal must have written the book. The spirit of freedom with which he wrote the book is proof of his mastery over his craft. The subject matter of the novel seems to have been a constant pleasure for Stendhal. He wrote without having to take sides with any of the characters. For this reason, for this *désinvolture* on the part of the novelist, which Gide felt in reading *La Chartreuse de Parme,* he placed it first in his list of the ten greatest French novels.

It took only a little under two months, in the year 1838, when he was living in Paris, for Stendhal to write *La Chartreuse.* Viewed in a schematic sense, it is a new version of *Le Rouge et le Noir.* Fabrice dreams first of being a military man and then turns to the priesthood, whereas Julien went first to the seminary and then, shortly before his death received an officer's commission. The two principal women characters have the same temperamental differences: a gentle tenderness in one and violent passionate feelings in the other, which Mme. de Rênal and Mathilde incarnate in *Le Rouge et le Noir.* But there are differences in structure and political significance. *Le Rouge* is more unified thanks to the continuous focus of interest in Julien Sorel. Fabrice is not at all times the central figure in *La Chartreuse.* Mosca, the most adroit of courtiers and the most lacking in moral rectitude, often occupies the first place in the novel's action. The small Italian court of the early nineteenth century has less political and sociological significance for today's readers than the political moment of the Restoration, analyzed in *Le Rouge et le Noir*.

The two novels reveal the same perceptiveness of Stendhal's psychological analysis. The small court of Parma is beautifully evoked and Fabrice as prisoner in the Farnese tower is a striking portrait. But by far the most intriguing and brilliantly developed theme is Gina's love for the nephew she raised. Gina's love for Fabrice, in its extraordinary complexity, is Stendhal's most masterful literary creation: a love that is both maternal and passionate and that turns into a jealous love when Gina realizes Fabrice is in love with Clélia. Up to the last page of the book, Gina's love is chaste and unarticulated. No one, not even Proust, has analyzed with such deftness and subtlety a love compounded so evenly of pathos in its deeply human aspect and of monstrousness in its social aspect.

La Chartreuse de Parme is perhaps a fuller testament of Stendhal than *Le Rouge et Le Noir,* because Stendhal is in both the young Fabrice and the older Mosca. He gave to Fabrice the beauty and the amorous exploits he never had, and to Mosca he gave the philosophy he hoped he could develop for himself. In killing off Fabrice, Stendhal hoped that he could survive in Mosca who becomes, at the end, the hero of the book, a fraternally close figure to Stendhal. Fabrice is a more refined, more socially graceful Julien. But he suffers from the same unrest, the same dissatisfaction with life, the same aspiration toward unknowable goals. Fabrice is supported by social connections and he is encouraged by countless social circumstances, but he is constantly driven on and tormented by dreams of some higher destiny. Favored by a maximum number of opportunities and successful in many of his encounters and projects, Fabrice does not reach

the happiness he wants. Disillusionments and disappointments characterize his life story more than triumphs. In having Mosca survive Fabrice, Stendhal seems to be ascribing to
the older man that kind of intelligence that adjusts to reality,
that makes compromises and treaties with the way of the
world. It is the stage of man's behavior that follows youth,
that sustains dreams, but that has learned how to dominate
the passions of love and the blind madness of jealousy. Mosca
has learned a great deal about the instability and the changeableness of passionate love, and he has chosen to replace
it with a more enduring kind of affection. He has replaced
sexual desire with a fervent kind of human sympathy. He
became the diplomat of the heart as well as the diplomat in
the politics of government. It is of course impossible to
measure the degree to which Stendhal projected himself into
the failures of Fabrice as consolation for his own failures,
and into the moderately peaceful triumphs of Mosca as
dreams of the accomplishment of his personal philosophy.
The melancholy that comes from such trials and failures and
compromises in the careers of Fabrice and Mosca is of such
a nature that it can be apprehended and felt by those sympathetic readers, by those *happy few* Stendhal had in mind
when he wrote this novel, where the search for happiness
turns to a form of resignation.

Between 1836 and 1839, Stendhal examined a large number of Italian chronicles. One of them in particular delighted
him. *Origine delle grandezze della famiglia Farnese.* On
August 16, 1838, he began work on a short story based on the
Farnese family. By September 3, he had decided to convert
the short story into a short novel—he used the word *roman-
zetto*—whose action would take place in modern times. The
principal clues of *La Chartreuse* are in this historical docu-

ment: Fabrice del Dongo is Alessandro Farnese, La Sanseverina is Vandozza, Count Mosca is Roderic, the Farnese
Tower is the Saint-Ange château, Clélia Conti is Cleria.
Other clues are still being discovered and suggested by scholars. The exact place in Paris where Stendhal wrote the book
was probably the rue Caumartin, and he spent not more
than seven weeks in November and December in the writing
of the novel. It was a feverish regimen of dictation and writing averaging twenty-three pages a day. He claimed that each
morning he read two or three pages in the Napoleonic law
book (*Le Code Civil*) in order to put himself in the right
state of mind and prepare himself for the correct style (*pour
prendre le ton*). If these details are accurate, *La Chartreuse
de Parme* is one of the most swiftly composed literary master-
pieces. Everything that Stendhal cherished most in the world
was poured into it: landscapes and music of his beloved
Italy, love romances, the analysis of passion, the study of
noble characters who were complex and fiery in their instincts and in their social roles.

The day after completing *La Chartreuse,* Stendhal gave
the manuscript to Colomb, who sold it to the publisher
Ambroise Dupont. The book, in two volumes, went on sale
at the end of March. Balzac, who was almost twenty years
younger than Stendhal, paid particular attention to the novel
and wrote in a letter to Mme. Hanska that Beyle had published the most beautiful book to appear in the last fifty
years, a novel the like of which Machiavelli would have
written if he had written novels. The following year, July
1840, in an article on Eugène Sue, Balzac referred to *La
Chartreuse de Parme* and congratulated Stendhal for the
way in which he had described the battle of Waterloo
(*décrivant Waterloo par le petit côté*). Balzac prophesied
that in time the book would be given more praise and im-

portance. In the same magazine (*La Revue Parisienne*), Balzac published, on September 25, his famous article on Stendhal, one of the very infrequent homages to Stendhal, and which moved the writer deeply. In his letter of reply to the article, Stendhal pointed out that many of the passages were the original dictations, unaltered, that he tended not to go back to the manuscript to make changes, that the style he preferred was underwritten rather than overwritten.

The opening sentence of the novel is the joining of France and Italy, the arrival of Napoleon in Milan, on May 15, 1796. It is Stendhal's celebration of the advent of a successor, after so many centuries, to Caesar and Alexander. With an almost reckless alacrity, Stendhal describes the French soldiers settling down in Milan. A lieutenant named Robert was assigned to the palace of the Marquise del Dongo. Both the marquise and the very young sister of her husband, Gina, who is to become Countess Pietranera (La Sanseverina) are attracted to the handsome French lieutenant. By the time the French are expelled from Milan, the marquise gives birth to a son, Fabrice, who does not resemble his legal father the marquis. This second son, Fabrice, conceived at the time of Milan's enthusiasm for Bonaparte, becomes the joy of his young aunt Gina. In opposition to his aged father's hatred for everything French, Fabrice grows up in a worship of Napoleon and freedom. When the news reaches him of Napoleon's return from Elba, he sees an eagle circling in the sky. It is a portent for him. He makes up his mind to cross Switzerland and join one of Napoleon's regiments.

The tone of the novel is set by this prelude scene of young Fabrice at the battle of Waterloo. The background is always grave political realities, and the foreground is the depiction of a youth's discovery of the world, of his surprise at the first encounters with the world's grimness, and his invincible lightness of heart that allows him to step aside and forget, at least momentarily, the fate of violence that hangs over Europe.

The first fifty pages narrate matters that Stendhal remembered hearing about in his seventeenth year: the spectacular social life in Milan after Marengo, followed by the story of Waterloo, not told as a chronological panorama of battle strategy, but as a series of fragmentary impressions observed by a witness. In 1815 Fabrice yearns to fight in Napoleon's army, as close as possible to his hero. He is able to leave Milan and reach the French army in Belgium on the day of the decisive battle. There is no time for him to enroll in the army. He belongs to no French regiment, but he finds a uniform and on the morning of June 18 starts out in the direction of the cannon fire. A canteen woman (*cantinière*) takes pity on his youthfulness and his bewilderment. She serves as a guide until he finds himself in the midst of some horsemen who were accompanying a marshal. Whenever Fabrice encounters someone, he asks, where is the battle? The surprising answer always is: You are in the midst of it! He is disappointed in seeing only smoke and trees that block his view of the horizon. He sees soldiers shooting at an invisible enemy, a corpse in the grass, a group of willows cut down by a cannon ball. When evening comes, he is caught up in a rout and forced along as far as Charleroi without seeing a single Englishman, without seeing the Emperor and without ever understanding what was happening around him.

Fabrice's boundless enthusiasm always wins out over the trials that beset him personally and that beset the world around him. There is an almost comic contrast between

Fabrice's belief in the legendary greatness of Napoleon and the Grande Armée, in the heroic exploits of battles, and in the realistic details he sees on the Italian roads: the stench of corpses, the soldiers' habit of stealing boots from the corpses. Fabrice spends a day simply trying to find his regiment. Every time he asks a question, he is growled at by some officer. His horse is stolen, and he begins to wonder if it is a real battle he is in. All trace of the bravery and heroism Fabrice had harbored in his dreams about war disappears. Canteen women and dead soldiers and peasants are robbed, and the robbers are those men whom Fabrice had once imagined would be his companions in arms. The most disheartening spectacle of all is the night scene where the soldiers, invisible, turn into men fleeing for their lives, cursing and showing their way in between wagons and cannon.

But these opening passages of *La Chartreuse* are always the scene observed by Fabrice. Stendhal never indulges in any comments of his own, never yields to any temptation to paint an elegant picture. The details and the general tone are all controlled by Fabrice's innocence and inexperience, by the freshness of his impressions. At the beginning and at the end of the scene, all the reader knows is the barest notation on Fabrice's temperament: an innate courage, a tendency to superstition, tireless enthusiasm and curiosity for what he encounters and a worship of Napoleon. Stendhal the novelist never invades or contaminates this freshness of outlook of his hero.

The heart and the movements of Fabrice are grace itself. The only question that troubles him is whether he is in a real battle or not. At one moment he is amazed to find himself just a few feet away from Marshal Ney. It is a momentous occasion, but Fabrice's only thought is that Ney has blond hair and that he, because his hair is light brown, will never be as brave as Ney. *Moi qui suis si pâle et qui ai des cheveux châtains, je ne serai comme ça . . . ces paroles voulaient dire: Jamais je ne serai un héros.* We never cease following the battle of Waterloo through the eyes of a teenager. The details chosen and invented by Stendhal, some pathetic and some comic, are details and thoughts that would occur to Fabrice in the unfolding of such an action on the day and the night he finds himself in the battle of Waterloo. Stendhal's art is the expression of these details, one rapidly following the other, until the scene becomes totally credible and the reader is absorbed in it.

From the very beginning, the lyric quality, the style of the entire work is established. We hear it as we can hear the beginning of a Mozart symphony. Stendhal communicates a joy and an eagerness as he composes and invents his world. He prepares the reader's mind and imagination to accept the world he is creating in the subtle combining of so many elements, no one of which is overstressed: the story of action, the analysis of the motives in the characters, the irony of human lives that meet and separate and meet again, the light that is diffused over all the scenes that is just sufficient to whet our appetites and to rivet our attention on what is transpiring.

But the prelude is not yet fully constituted. Only the first theme has been developed—the joyous temperament of Fabrice, the happiness he finds in enthusiasm itself. It is in his desire to join Napoleon's army, in the lightness of his heart, in the ingenuousness with which he lived through the day and the night of the 18th of June. Before the really serious part of the novel's action begins, that is, before Fabrice returns to Milan, he is going to demonstrate, in his first meeting with Clélia Conti, the second theme of the prelude, richer and more pervasive than the first, namely the same ingenuousness and sparkle of spirit fused with some degree of peril.

On June 19, Fabrice reaches the inn of L'Etrille, in the Flemish village of Zonders, where he stays for two weeks to recover from his wounds. From there he goes to Amiens where he remains two weeks in July. In August he goes to Paris and from there to Geneva where he learns that in Milan he has been denounced to the police as a French sympathizer by his own elder brother Ascagne, the *marchesino,* a man of arrogant civic pride. After a few days of concealed sojourn in the castle of Grianta, Fabrice reaches Milan where he settles down in precautionary secrecy. During this elaborate moving about the first meeting between Fabrice and the young girl Clélia Conti takes place, in an atmosphere of romance, sensuality, happiness and the ominous threat of imprisonment.

Young women in summer dresses, in an open carriage, with Fabrice in their company, are stopped by Austrian police. They have orders to arrest General Fabio Conti and they mistake Fabrice for him. The scene becomes an *opéra bouffe* of mistaken identities. General Conti, the father of Clélia, is in the group, but dressed in civilian clothes. Nothing is ever clarified but the members of the group follow their instincts and make a kind of *déjeuner sur l'herbe.* Wine and food are found in a nearby farm. Clélia, a young girl of twelve, senses that Fabrice has performed somewhere heroically and watches him slyly with admiration.

The entire scene—composed of sunlight and a poetic landscape, swift in the unfolding of its action and overcast by the danger of a political order—brings to a close the elaborate prologue-introduction in which many of the characters are introduced and the tone set for the novel that is to follow. Fabrice is going to spend a few years in a small town in one of the papal states. There he will simply wait for matters to clear up. There he will attend mass every day and lead the kind of bland existence that will make him appear the opposite of what he is in the opening scenes: a youthful genius, a charmer and a conspirator.

Fabrice's first encounter with Clélia Conti announces the passion they will feel for one another, a love that will constitute the center of the novel. But this love is never neglected for the other two romantic stories in the book, two loves that are more mysterious, more ambiguous, more deeply sensuous: that of Duchess Sanseverina for her handsome nephew Fabrice and that of Count Mosca for La Sanseverina.

If, before looking at the various peripeteia of the book, we look at the general plan, Fabrice del Dongo stands out as the protagonist of *La Chartreuse* because he is at the heart of all of these adventures of ardor and love. In terms of the book's action, he escapes from his sentence and from prison, thanks to the combined intrigues and interventions of Clélia and Sanseverina. Thanks to their devotion, Fabrice can look forward to reaching the highest ecclesiastical rank. Clélia, married against her will, dies after giving birth to the son she conceived with Fabrice. As a result of these events, Fabrice retires into a Carthusian monastery (*une chartreuse*) where he dies soon afterward. This monastery provides the title for the novel. It is a book that combines many fictional forms: a novel of adventure, romance, history, psychology. It is perhaps more than any other form, a novel of extraordinarily sustained lyricism. For those readers who are strongly attracted to the man Stendhal, to his character, his life and his art, *La Chartreuse de Parme* is an autobiography, the most transparent of a totally transposed autobiography.

The role of the priest in Europe, after the fall of Napoleon, is a major theme in both *Le Rouge et le Noir* and *La Chartreuse de Parme*. The type of young man, Julien or Fabrice, exhilarated by the glory of military achievement, has to learn how to adjust his ambitions to ecclesiastical glory. Whatever form of ambition or power appealed to a young man around 1830, the inevitable advice given to him was: "enter the priesthood." After Julien's conquest of Mme. de Rênal, he has to accept the ways of the seminary and has no difficulty in adjusting his lack of religious belief to external religious exercises. After Fabrice's day at Waterloo and the multiple adventures that follow it immediately, the absence of any strict moral behavior in him (his amoralism, in a word) harmonizes with his fundamental and quite sincere religious beliefs. Fabrice would seem to be hypocritical but he is not, and he would seem to be ambitious, but actually he is fairly indifferent to ambition. These two traits, or these two absences of traits, hypocrisy and a deep sense of ambition, indicate a radical difference of character with Julien Sorel.

Almost before realizing it, we move quickly into the world of comedy in *La Chartreuse,* in the generalized spectacle of the tiny Italian kingdom, which because of its geographical and even temporal distance (the original spectacle came from the Renaissance) allows Stendhal to depict the world of his novel, without the bitterness that is often felt in *Le Rouge et le Noir*. It is the highest form of comedy, precisely that form, which according to the lights of a Molière, will depict the vices of mankind and give to the spectator the sense that he is being taught by the playwright to understand the weaknesses of man and to correct them in himself and in his

society. The secondary characters of *La Chartreuse,* especially, resemble characters of a high comedy of manners.
They are stock characters, but sufficiently individualized to
be memorable: for example, the grand duke of Parma,
Ranuce-Ernest IV, who affects the airs of a Louis XIV in his
seeming haughtiness, but who is actually terrified of an up-
rising in his kingdom. He is proud to be the ruler, but can
never totally forget that he rules over a tiny inconsequential
kingdom. He is fundamentally cruel by nature, but does
not dare exercise his cruelty. No traits of this character are
directly analyzed by Stendhal, but the minute flashes and details the novelist gives of Ranuce-Ernest provide an admirable portrait of a potentate whose prudence keeps him from
committing the worst crimes.

We follow the comedy of the tiny court, with its courtiers
and ruler; its prince who becomes a young king, terrified at
the discovery of the corruption around him, after spending
the years of his youth in the study of mineralogy; its General
Fabio Conti whose life loses all meaning at those times when
he receives no social invitations; and countless other characters. And we follow at the same time its relationship with the
drama of real governments and real politicians, a drama unarticulated by Stendhal but which his art, in the gallery of
his characters, calls up in the mind of the reader. The comic
scenes, or those that are at least partially comic, never exist
without their serious counterpart even if it is never explicitly stated. Behind the carnival effect of pomposity and deceit, there is the serious wonderment concerning the possibility of man reaching a greater degree of justice in government
and law. The word "comedy" is used at the end of the novel
by Count Mosca, the minister who at the beginning of his
career had worn the uniform of Napoleon's army in the
Spanish campaign and who finally dresses like a puppet of

the court: *je m'habille comme un personnage de comédie.*

When Fabrice returns to Lombardy, after his adventures in war, he seeks out his Aunt Gina for whom he feels an unusually warm affection. The relationship between nephew and aunt is mysterious and ambiguous from the novel's beginning to its end. If Fabrice had made love to her at the time of his return, she would doubtless have responded with passion. Gina was first married to Count Pietranera and at his death in the war entered upon a second marriage with an elderly duke, Sanseverina, who did not often force himself on her presence. The intimate relationship she has with Count Mosca, prime minister of the Prince of Parma, is a faithful relationship, but does not reach, on her part, any degree of exalted passion. When Gina urges Fabrice to enter the priesthood, we can easily guess that it is for the purpose of keeping him for herself, or at least for keeping him separated legally from any other woman. A delightful frankness characterizes Gina's relationship with Mosca, except for her references to Fabrice when she plans carefully what she says. Gina's very existence may account for Fabrice's inability to find any real happiness in his numerous love affairs.

The momentary pleasures Fabrice has in his sexual life does not seem in the least to affect his religious convictions. He remains a believer, unlike his creator Stendhal. The rather simple but stalwart religious faith of Fabrice is a psychological enrichment for the novel, and also the real but somewhat superstitious piety of Clélia Conti has its importance in Fabrice's love for her.

The action of the novel gravitates around a set of human relationships that are explored in some detail, without ever being lucidly defined. The trio of Gina, Fabrice, Mosca make up a trio of sentiments that grow and diminish and grow again, that almost reach the clarity of definition and announcement, but that, like a musical composition, continue in an ever-closer intermingling and wonderment. Mosca's jealousy, for example, might have reached a point of tragic drama, if Gina had ever named the sentiment that attracted her to Fabrice. But she never does, and Mosca remains impeccable in his behavior. His suffering over jealousy is never too profound. The turnings and twistings of Fabrice's emotions are the most tormented of the three characters. His attachment to his aunt is of such significance to him that he cannot alter it by feeling for her, and carrying it out, a sexual expression and involvement. He quite literally suffers from sexual impotence in the presence of Gina through fear of losing her love, of disappointing her if he ever attempted to make her his mistress. He fears that then she would doubt even the love without sex that attaches him to her. In the presence of Sanseverina, Fabrice appears as a boy in love, who has no experience of physical love and who is simply waiting for that moment when his senses will force him toward the climax he both wants and fears. Gina is love idealized for Fabrice. She is the mystical goal of love and not the woman. Fabrice suffers from the sickness of expectation, the sickness of waiting. He feels the ardor of love, without loving, and he suffers at times from that vague form of melancholy and even of anguish that his century named "romantic love."

Not until he is in prison, in the Farnese Tower, will Fabrice feel the intensity of that love he had always wanted to feel, and it will be for Clélia Conti. Before the sentiment becomes totally clear, it passes through the phases of that process Stendhal calls "crystallization." When it reaches its fullest degree of sincerity and vehemence, it is of such a nature that it makes him call for death and refuse any means of escape. *Je ne veux pas me sauver. Je veux mourir ici.* The moment is quite comparable, in its plenitude, to the final moment of Julien Sorel and the happiness he feels with Mme. de Rênal in his prison. For Stendhal, the hero's happiness coincides with his death or at least with his death wish. The vicissitudes of life, and especially those vicissitudes of a youth whose ambition is clear and arduous, form a continuous series of obstacles not only to happiness, but to a lucid picture of happiness.

Gina's complex nature often recalls Mathilde de la Mole, and at the end of the novel, when she serves Fabrice so selflessly and so efficaciously, she plays the almost identical role of Mathilde for Julien, when her help is not even acknowledged by Fabrice, when all of his thoughts are concentrated on Clélia. Gina has all the varied traits of character that form a rich personality: wit, beauty, willfulness, charm, vindictiveness, determination. When she fears that Fabrice will be poisoned in his cell, she does her utmost to arrange means for his escape. He gives his consent to Gina's plans only when Clélia asks for it also. Fabrice's character has changed and deepened, but in his feelings for Gina he has not changed. For her, he is still the lighthearted libertine, in search of love, who is incapable of loving her in the way she would wish.

The complicated moves necessary for Fabrice's escape from prison are related to the psychological complexities in the three characters. Fabrice manifests no really deep gratitude to Gina. He thanks her hastily, in conventional terms, and, although he does not speak of Clélia, Gina knows that her rival has his love. Moreover, Clélia's help was necessary for the success of Gina's steps in the liberation of

Fabrice. The prison maneuvers recapitulate all the emotional intricacies of the book. Fabrice stands between the two women who love him, as Julien Sorel stood between Mathilde and Louise de Rênal at the end of *Le Rouge et le Noir*.

It is an extraordinary quartet: Fabrice and Mosca, Gina and Clélia, whose emotions and feelings are revealed slowly and patiently by Stendhal, the kind of writer who never takes recourse to any obvious, offensive and strident analysis. It is as if the novelist felt respect for the most intimate feelings of his characters or at least deemed himself inadequate in his understanding.

In his art of novelist, Stendhal's triumph is perhaps in his portrait of Gina. The love she feels for Fabrice is of such a nature and develops under such peculiar circumstances, that she never to herself quite acknowledges what it is. Stendhal's tact in his treatment of Gina is totally noble. Her struggle is with herself. The erotic sensuality she feels for Fabrice— and every sensitive reader of *La Chartreuse de Parme* is aware of these feelings in her—has to be meted out in forms of devotion and solicitude. Her love is constantly being discouraged from revealing itself, so it appears disguised, and Gina conceals from herself, as best she can, her humiliations. The boundless energy she has and the absence of moral and social prejudice in her nature give support to the years when she lives with her love and is unable to acknowledge it to herself or to Fabrice. She is, quite simply, an extraordinary woman: not as maternally tender as Mme. de Rênal, older in her wisdom of the heart and in her fortitude of character than Mathilde de la Mole, but combining Mme. de Rênal's power of devotion and Mathilde's instinctive passion. For what reason does she love Fabrice? For the nobility of his character, for his courage and for his beauty or for what she would call his gracefulness. In a disarmingly simple way she once says to Mosca, in speaking of Fabrice, that unless he were happy, she could not be happy. *Enfin, s'il n'est heureux, je ne puis être heureuse.* This aphoristic sentence is the clue to Gina's feelings and to her actions.

The slow development of love in Clélia Conti's heart is a moving illustration of Stendhal's "crystallization." As it grows, it becomes more and more demanding. As it becomes more passionate, it becomes purer in the sense that it becomes all loves in one. It is so total that it can contain a sense of pity for Fabrice and a sense of compassion for Gina. It can even be colored by jealousy and a sentiment that is close to hatred for Gina. Clélia gives herself to Fabrice when she believes he has been poisoned. On the insistence of her father, she marries the Marquis Crescenzia. When Fabrice is elevated to the post of Archbishop of Parma, he knows he is again in the power of Clélia and desires her again despite his resolutions. He preaches regularly in the cathedral and with marked success. During one of his sermons, he sees Clélia in the front row of the congregation and is unable to continue the sermon. He reads a prayer that is destined for her, and that text, like the book that united Paolo and Francesca, brings Clélia and Fabrice again together. Clélia had once made a vow to the Virgin never to have sexual relationships again with Fabrice when he would be visible to her. She receives him only in the dark and refuses to look at him. The baby boy Sandrino that is born to them dies almost immediately, but Fabrice feels for him the same love that Julien Sorel felt for the son he was to have by Mathilde. Clélia survives her son by only a few months. The ending of the novel is a series of deaths. Fabrice dies in the Charter House of Parma where he has withdrawn from the world. Gina, who has become Countess Mosca, dies also, but not before she accepts the advances of the new prince. She does this solely for the purpose of saving Fabrice.

Count Mosca has the sense of honor, the courtliness, and the profoundly human qualities of the ideal knight. His role of diplomat could easily have lent itself to ridicule, but Stendhal never ridicules his character. Mosca knows the disillusionments of life, but lives with them stoically, patiently. At the end of the novel, where the action is swift and the emotions more tense than elsewhere, Count Mosca is the only one of the principal characters who does not die. He is the only one of the quartet able to withstand such bereavement, able to live through the sadness of death and absence. The final brief paragraph of *La Chartreuse de Parme* is a supremely ironic commentary on the tumultuous scenes we have read: the prisons are empty (and we think of the prison where Fabrice knew happiness), the count is lavishly wealthy (and we think of how little this fact would mean to Mosca), and the subjects of the new prince Ernest V think highly of his government (and we remember that this miniature Italian court was the setting of the universally human drama that is now over and henceforth consigned "to the happy few"). *Les prisons de Parme étaient vides, le comte immensément riche, Ernest V adoré de ses sujets qui comparaient son gouvernement à celui des grands-ducs de Toscane.*

No one of the Stendhal characters in *La Chartreuse* believes with any degree of faith in the political and social situation where he finds himself. And yet no one of them ever reaches the degree of pessimism and despair concerning the government and society that Julien Sorel felt. They are of another lineage, of an aristocracy trained in the ways of stoicism and pride and who fall back on themselves and on their secret dream of happiness. More than the charac-

ters of *Le Rouge et le Noir,* those of *La Chartreuse* have an
exceptional disposition for happiness. Their search for happiness, for *le bonheur* as Stendhal understood it, is more
deliberate and more joyous than in any other of his books.
Their very understanding of one another is a form of happiness, the sympathy and tenderness their natures show,
their appreciation of the beautiful landscapes they look at,
their wit and gaiety springing forth naturally when they are
together in groups, the courage they all demonstrate whenever they are together in groups, the courage they all demonstrate whenever there is need for courage, the satisfaction
that comes to them from very slight things such as the exchange of smiles and glances. All of this is the pattern of
happiness. It is composed out of fragile matters: the almost
chance encounters with one another or a simple walk in the
woods. The drastic happenings that keep occurring never
succeed in extinguishing the flashes of happiness that illu-
minate the novel. Friendship, love, understanding and an
almost permanent form of sexual attraction, even if it is not
indulged, are the spiritual bonds uniting these four characters who in themselves, in the ever-forming and reforming
relationships they make with one another, create a world
apart from the world of the Italian court and apart from
their century. They believe in themselves, even if they are
unable to believe in ideas and politics and human ideals.
Injustice takes over everything except the concealed kingdom of their hearts. Their happiness and their isolation are
subtle manifestations of what Stendhal calls "egotism."

Such a term as egotism is shocking when it is applied to
such figures as Clélia and Gina, Fabrice and Mosca. It is
shocking because their human qualities and nobility are
such that the reader forgets the starkness of some of their
acts. It is difficult to think of Clélia as the girl who has a

child by her bishop or to remember that Gina is the publicly acknowledged mistress of the prime minister, that Fabrice is a priest using his ministry to secure sexual favors
and that Mosca betrays the trust of his superior. The strict
code of morality has been replaced by a code of egotism,
namely, a code of duty toward oneself and of duty toward
those one loves. The egotism of Fabrice and Mosca is at
times expressed by acts of violence and even murder, but it
is often altered into a form of lighthearted indifference toward the world, into an absence of solicitude that sets them
off from other men. But such moods of *désinvolture* do not
last for long. Fundamentally Fabrice and Mosca are not hard
or indifferent. They are attached to humanity, to its beauty
and to the suffering that humanity endures. Fabrice, somewhat more than Mosca, feels in countless small episodes a
warm affection for the little people of his country, for the
obscure Italians who themselves have an instinctive love for
life and for one another.

Both Gina and Mosca demonstrate the same Franciscan-
like love for humanity, but they are older than Fabrice, and
their feelings are more tempered by skepticism. Fabrice in
this respect is a younger, more vulnerable and more emotional Mosca and Gina. They instinctively love those members of the human race who are not associated with laws
and government. But for the minority, the lawgivers and the
rulers, they demonstrate a very definite loathing. They themselves never articulate their differing attitudes toward these
two divisions of humanity: the people and those in authority.
But the difference is clear in their actions and reactions.
They move easily back and forth between feelings of scorn
and feelings of affection. A small segment of humanity is
for them the enemy, and in opposing such an enemy there
are quite simply no restrictions. The one in authority is

looked upon instinctively as a monster under whose stric-
ture and whims anything is possible. Whereas Balzac describes in blatant rhetorical terms the ferocity and the hypocrisy of men, especially of those men in power, Stendhal
makes us feel that ferocity and hypocrisy in the reactions of
Mosca and Fabrice and Gina, in what they say and what they
do. This theme in Stendhal is expressed not as a lesson or
as a sermon, but as an integral part in daily living, in the
instinctive feelings of fear and hate that rise up in the hearts
of those who naturally love mankind.

On one occasion, Mosca in a conversation with Fabrice
compares the strategy that has to be used when living at
court to a game of whist and the rules that one automatically
accepts when one plays whist. Even if Mosca has no respect
for the prince, he will accept favors and privileges from the
prince as belonging to him in accordance with the rules of
the game. During the time that Fabrice is serving his sentence as a political prisoner, when therefore his life is in
constant danger, Mosca and Gina continue to lead their
life in court, in a seemingly peaceful manner, while they
plot to discover means by which Fabrice may escape.

The courtier is not a revolutionist. His plotting against
the ruler, or against an edict of the ruler, is part of the accepted court etiquette. A *carbonaro* is the outside fighter
and has no relationship with a Mosca whose opposition to
the government is in reality his scorn for the government.
Whereas Julien Sorel has the makings of a real revolutionist,
Fabrice does not. In *La Chartreuse de Parme* the sentiments
of the young protagonist Fabrice and of his counterpart, the
older protagonist Mosca, are so formed by a sense of modesty
and a sense of honor, that any blatant act, such as an upris-
ing or a revolution, would be unthinkable. No matter how
deficient or corrupt the government is, there is within its

confines an oasis where men of good will and generous spirit may live together and share the pleasure of friendship and cultivate the hope for happiness. On every level of the book's construction, in every episode where the leading characters come together, in the moments of tense crisis and the moments of relaxed gaiety, *La Chartreuse de Parme* is the narrative of man's search for happiness. It is evident in the pathos of the book, in the humorous scenes, in the ironical scenes of courtly behavior and courtly deceit, in the countless episodes where love is disguised, partly disguised or passionately revealed.

The variety of themes in *La Chartreuse,* the variety of tones and moods and the absence of any rigorous construction tend to encourage the reader to follow the narrative as a series of episodes in a picaresque novel. But consciously at times and subconsciously at all other times, Stendhal is writing a novel on the search for happiness, and it is precisely this motif that gives to the work its depth and its most abiding significance.

It is this theme that preeminently designates Fabrice as a protagonist, as the central figure who mysteriously draws into his presence all the other figures of the story. Julien, in his aloneness, is Stendhal's tragic hero, but Fabrice is not alone. He is seen with other characters where his charm, his beauty and his courage are forces drawing the others to him, forces he himself exploits in order to create a pattern of human relationship that may give him some sense of approaching that goal of happiness he does not always need to articulate because it is always ahead of him. Julien is fundamentally alone, and at all times lives in a state of alert, even when he is with Mme. de Rênal and Mathilde, and more so with all the other characters in *Le Rouge et le Noir:* with his father, with M. de Rênal, with M. de la Mole, with

Valenod. But Fabrice shares his life and his feelings and his thoughts with others. He exists beside someone else and in some form of relationship with that person. With very little encouragement, he confides easily with those he encounters, as if the world, or the world he knows, has been relieved of all traces of original sin, of all traces of corruption. He gives no evidence of feeling scorn for society or for any class of society, and he has to be reminded that most people do feel and express scorn for others. His very presence engenders a kind of joy in those he meets. He is the only Stendhal character who has this power and he is therefore the most brilliant and the most subtle exponent of Stendhalian happiness.

The boy discovering the world and marveling at it, whom we follow about in the opening scene at Waterloo, is basically Fabrice of the entire book. There are moments he spends with Marietta and with Gina, which could not literally be called moments of love, but more simply brief impressions of being alive and delighting in what he finds in life. At such moments he resembles a young puppy rolling on the ground and enjoying the pats and the caresses he is given. Happiness may be composed of very little, of not much more than the pure sensation of being alive. Fabrice is impervious to all possible threats and perils: to police and customs men, to soldiers and to an armed assailant, to prison. He plays with the dog of one of his jailers and practically becomes a friend of his jailers. His imprisonment fails to depress him because from the top of his tower he can see out over the plain of the Po River and beyond that to the foothills of the Alps in the distance.

Fabrice has the disposition for happiness that Julien did not have. The dangers encountered at Waterloo and in prison are quite literally for Fabrice experiences to be en-

joyed. He is curious about them and will never allow the
wickedness of men to alter his permanent vision of life as
something to be enjoyed in all its aspects. His courage is
perhaps a little less than courage. It is more a sense of confidence in life, a confidence in his own fate. The testing of
this principle (which is more an instinct than a principle)
is Fabrice's ability to find in prison itself his deepest experience of happiness. Over and over again, Fabrice illustrates
the belief that man's immediate care or worry or danger is
not as important as his spirit, which is able to move freely
beyond the care and the worry and the danger.

How is Fabrice able to sustain this spirit of freedom, this
légèreté? By avoiding any serious and specific involvement
with any of the characters in the novel, except with Clélia
at the end. He is infinitely more concerned with happiness
than with any attempt to become a high dignitary in the
Church. When the elevation does come, he accepts it easily
and almost with indifference. Fabrice lives in a spirit of *in-
souciance* that Julien Sorel never knows. With good reason,
Julien calculates every move he makes, whereas Fabrice,
with good reason also, is able to live casually with what
comes his way, with those chances of fate that by right belong to a young nobleman.

Around all the moves of Julien, so carefully planned by
him and analyzed by him after they have been carried out,
Stendhal the novelist creates a very intense atmosphere of
pathos. Fabrice's freedom of spirit and freedom of movement prevent the forming of any such pathos in *La Chartreuse de Parme.* Here the novelist seems to watch his
hero with admiration rather than with pity. From the very
beginning of the novel Stendhal knows, and the reader
knows also, that if Fabrice really wants to wear the bishop's
purple, his wish will be granted and without too much effort

on his part. Even at the most melodramatic moments of his life, at the time of the fight with Giletti and the subsequent escape from justice, when wounded in his leg and shoulder, Fabrice bears a protective charm. He is eternally *romanesque* in the sense that he always poetizes danger and exploits such circumstances as ways to demonstrate his ingenuousness, his physical and spiritual litheness that enables him to transcend danger. He creates his life effortlessly, whereas Julien forges his life with infinite pain and succumbs to a defeat of which he was at all times conscious.

Stendhal enjoys the spectacles provided by Fabrice without ever judging them. In the boy's character waves of enthusiasm vie with deep-seated superstitions. An idea occurs to him, and in most cases the following out of the idea seems to have little connection with it. As the creator of the fictional character Fabrice del Dongo, Stendhal has him move about swiftly and often inconsequentially in a manner that resembles Jean-Luc Godard's technique in his films, in *Pierrot le fou*, for example, or *Masculin-Féminin*, where the giddiness of the hero is part of his charm, and where the freshness of youth is photographed against the predictable gestures and stolidness of middle age. Only in the final chapters does Fabrice enter upon another phase which might be called maturity when his instinctive joviality is covered over by the real beginnings of suffering. But up until the final chapters of *La Chartreuse*, Fabrice is the figure always escaping from predicaments and emotions, a Candide or a Belmondo in *Pierrot le fou*. He is no one being, he is the spirit of a being, as enchanting as he is elusive. He is detached from all specific pleasures of life and from all ordinary ambitions in life. He creates the order of the moment that he will soon leave behind in the creation of a new order. How opened he is to life and how vulnerable! He understands the world because he does not try to understand it and codify it. The seemingly insignificant things that Fabrice enjoys—sounds in nature, brief emotions of the heart —could not be enjoyed by others, by those who are precisely involved in calculations and preparations, in stratagems and campaigns of deceit. He is the ever-fresh spirit in the midst of all that.

It would be difficult to depict and to project such a character as Fabrice without a clear setting. The care with which Stendhal evokes the court of Parma is proof of his understanding of this need. Such a character as Fabrice, and of course the others also, Gina and Mosca in particular, have to move about within a world. They have to be seen in a world and bound to it in countless ways. The political dimensions of the book are everywhere visible and measurable. The actions of such a figure as Mosca are those of a statesman who, in meting out power to this one and that one, knows the consequences, knows the various plottings that his decision will affect. Political maneuvering in a small state is not unlike that of a large state. In his praise of *La Chartreuse de Parme*, Balzac stressed the admirable qualities of Mosca's speech and actions, and compared them to the profundity of La Rochefoucauld's *Maximes*.

What is the general structure of the novel? After the prelude containing allusions to the mysterious birth of Fabrice and the day at Waterloo in which he unwittingly meets his real father, Lieutenant Robert, the first half of the novel is in large part the elaborate background of the court of Parma as seen principally through the life of Mosca and Gina. Slightly before the actual middle of the book occurs a seemingly insignificant episode: the fight between Fabrice and Giletti in which Giletti is killed. It is a brief story of jealousy and violence, the typical subject matter of a *fait divers*. But the scene turns out to be the central crisis of the novel.

Everything that preceded this quarrel prepared it: Fabrice's attention to women, his seductiveness, his agility and courage and physical strength, his pride too and his sense of superiority. And everything that follows the Fabrice–Giletti quarrel is the result of it. A complicated plot sets in motion countless characters who are all engaged, in some way or other, in the search for justice, in the necessary political moves to achieve immediate and distant ends. Here again, Balzac especially admired the skill with which Stendhal carried forward a complicated plot involving so many characters. He sees *La Chartreuse* as that type of novel for which he had a marked predilection: a drama with one hundred characters, clearly organized and based upon political reality. Stendhal, in his answer to this article, felt that Balzac was imposing on *La Chartreuse* patterns of a novel and rules of fictional art that had not been apparent to Stendhal when he was composing the work. Very possibly those qualities of *La Chartreuse de Parme* that are the most admired today had not been apparent to Balzac when he read the novel and tried to see in it a novel *à la* Walter Scott.

It is much more. It is the story of a young Italian nobleman (whose real father was French) who, after 1815, leads a life of adventure and passion, in a country where there are as many signs of corruption as there are signs of heroism, where there are as many episodes inciting fear as there are episodes inspiring a love for life. As the son of an Italian countess and recognized as his son by Count del Dongo, Fabrice's existence would normally be easygoing and superficial. But it is impossible for him to lead such an existence, because of the vitality and strong character of his aunt Gina

Pietranera and her friend Count Mosca. They support him in his desire to lead a more dangerous existence at an historical moment not at all suitable for a dangerous existence.

These three characters, Fabrice, Gina and Mosca, are fundamentally passionate and disinterested. Each one is capable of shrewdness and calculation, but each one is at the same time scornful of such behavior. Their thoughts and their actions make the novel into two novels: an epic poem on the joy that can be found in living and the epic story of a society. The court of Parma prolongs in its own way the battle of Waterloo, and the description of the French army arriving in Italy in 1796, which is the theme of the opening chapters. For the simple reason that Fabrice had taken his stand beside Napoleon in 1814, political hatred will be directed toward him much later in the book. The protagonist looks upon himself as an adventurer and as a former *bonapartiste*. This is sufficient to convert the tiny principality of Parma into a battlefield. Fabrice's life is forced to take on heroic proportions. His fate was decided at the battle of Waterloo. He will be helped and supported by a few noble souls, but he will be opposed by the envy, the anger and the jealousy of many others.

The novel is a manhunt—the initial movement of which unfolds in close proximity to Napoleon himself—that terminates in prison. And yet the novel is not essentially one of adventure. It is a study of passion, a genre that the French would call *un roman passionnel*.

After Waterloo Fabrice, in the eyes of his aunt Gina, takes on the proportions of a hero. She sees him as a man she could love and, without clearly recognizing it, she begins to love him. Fabrice's passion for Napoleon is transferred to Gina's passion for Fabrice. The impossibility of acknowledging this love to herself and to others forces her to accept

the attentions of Count Mosca, who is able to convince her
that in order to protect her nephew at court she should
marry Duke Sanseverina.

The strong sensuality of Fabrice's nature leads him from
one amorous adventure to another, while the unspoken love
of Gina for him waits in the background. One day, when he
is actually on the way to prison, he meets a young girl Clélia,
daughter of General Fabio Conti, governor of the citadel of
Parma. With this encounter, the structure of the novel is
visible. Fabrice, endowed with beauty and charm, attracts to
him the three figures of Mosca, Gina and Clélia. In varying
degrees of fidelity and passion, these three characters are
attached to the ardor of his spirit and his physical attrac-
tiveness. They are moved by the dynamics of his movements.
He welcomes their advice and receives multiple favors from
them. He becomes their creation, their pupil, as he learns
from them, from Mosca and Gina in particular, the rules of
social behavior, the complex stratagems of court life. He
studies at the Ecclesiastical Institute of Naples, and later,
when he is on the point of being elevated to archbishop, his
success as a prelate and preacher is such that he can openly
demonstrate a disapproval of court life. When, as a very
young man, he wore for the first time the purple stockings,
sign of his priestly vocation, Gina gave him important advice that he always followed: Never to shine in a conversation
when the opportunity presents itself, but to remain silent
and allow the others to read his thoughts in his eyes.

Fabrice naturally and easily develops in himself the tone
and the spirit of the medieval lord, of *un grand seigneur*.
Before meeting Clélia and falling in love with her, in his
wilder period of seducer, he defends himself against Giletti,
the lover of his mistress Marietta, and kills the man. This is
exactly the act the *prepotenti* were waiting for. All those

hostile to Mosca's party at court had now the chance to avenge the haughtiness of Gina Pietranera and the power of Count Mosca. Fabrice is called by them an assassin and sent to the citadel.

But there, Fabrice, in his turn, is able to inspire in his aunt and his older friend Mosca the heroism and nobility of spirit that initially they had inspired in him. The new setting reveals Fabrice to himself and gradually reveals to him his love for Clélia Conti. From a window and a terrace Fabrice and Clélia compose by signs an alphabet which will permit them to exchange messages. At the end, Clélia betrays her father by becoming an accomplice in Fabrice's escape from prison.

At this point in the novel, each of the four characters reaches his highest form of nobility, by committing himself totally to a cause. Clélia accepts marriage with the Marquis Crescenzi without ever renouncing her secret vows to Fabrice. Gina and Mosca risk losing their position in order to help Fabrice, and at a moment when they know he is in love with Clélia and has therefore stopped thinking very much about them. And Fabrice, for the first time in his life, is deeply in love with one person.

This commitment of each of the four adds a new tone of gravity to the last chapters of *La Chartreuse*. The lovers are separated, but Fabrice, after his escape and after his elevation to archbishop, continues to preach with the hope that one day Clélia will come to hear him. This does happen, and Clélia, who had sworn never to see her lover again, receives him in the dark. Her conscience is quieted by this mental restriction. Love, once an erotic adventure for Fabrice, has now taken on the implacable seriousness of fate and imposes its rigor on Fabrice, on all his thoughts and actions. His religious duties are severe, but they are subordinated to his love for Clélia. Gina and Mosca, deprived of the immediate attention and affection of Fabrice, continue to be totally devoted to him.

The fundamental traits of these characters which were clear from the beginning: Fabrice's heroism, Gina's passion for life, and Mosca's hedonism—are all present at the end, but they have been deepened into sentiments that are more demanding, more rigorous, more "Corneilian," as the French would say. During the first half of the book, life is dangerous, and during the second half, life becomes serious when Stendhal demonstrates in the actions and thoughts of these characters so close to him in many ways, what he demanded of human nature, what he hoped would develop in human nature.

The four leading characters of *La Chartreuse de Parme* adjust to their moment in history and merge with the mores of their day far more naturally than the hero of *Le Rouge et le Noir*. It is a simpler matter to be a *révolté*, as Julien was, than to show greatness and generosity within a political-social context, as Fabrice does. Fabrice and Mosca, Gina and Clélia have in common an ardor that is never diminished by intrigue and ambition. Their ardor is of such a passionate nature that they are able at the great moments of decision to sacrifice everything to it. Their ardor withstands every attack of society and politics, every assault of meanness and envy. Ardor is their honor and their absolute. And this is, for Stendhal, the indispensable basis for happiness.

How is the unity of such a book maintained, where the episodes are narrated so swiftly and sketchily? The plot itself, to some degree, holds the various parts of the book together. The omens (such as the eagle seen flying in the direction of France) and the emblems (such as the tower, *la tour* Farnèse, on the top of the citadel of Parma), far more subtly than the plot, provide a secret and poetic unity for *La Chartreuse*. But more perhaps than these, it is Stendhal's presence in the narrative that gives it its unity and not merely the comments he as the omniscient novelist makes. It is in his relationship with the characters, his identification with them. He is, for example, the invisible father for Fabrice. His relationship with *la duchesse*, Sanseverina, is a loving admiration. With Mosca, where the bonds of identification are still closer, the admiration is not so loving, perhaps, as it is watchful and curious. Mosca is another self Stendhal studies, as he might study the works of a thoughtful writer. In their life of fictional characters, what these three characters admire was also admired by Stendhal.

Since his attention cannot always be fixed on these characters of his predilection, since, after all, he is a novelist and one of considerable scope in his two major works, he has to present the leading characters in relationship with other characters, and he creates them without exaggeration, without caricature: Abbé Blanès, General Conti, the Marquis Crescenzi, the *mamacia*, so protective of the young actress Marietta. A world comes to life in these characters and in many others: in Fabrice's brother, in the actress Fausta, in Archbishop Landriani, the jailer Grillo, in Ludovic. Each has his role, each speaks as the representative of his own particular world. Ludovic, for example, represents all of the servants of Gina Pietranera. When Fabrice gives his sermons in the church of Parma, the young girl Marina, appearing very briefly and falling in love with Fabrice, is representative of the women of Parma who are spiritually seduced by Fabrice and testify to his oratorical success.

Stendhal is more determinedly present in *La Chartreuse* than in his other books in the direct advice he offers and the demands he makes of the reader. This communication with the reader permits the novelist to pass rapidly over long periods of time he has no interest in narrating. Stendhal is transposing the story of a moment in Italian history, that of Vandozza Farnese, but his abundant use of omens and predictions (those of Fabrice about himself and those of Abbé Blanès) give the impression of constant improvization on the part of the novelist. The future of his characters is known, but it is revealed in a semipoetic way. The death, for example, of Fabrice's child is the image of a branch stripped from a tree.

It is known that Stendhal, on the demands of his publisher, shortened his novel rather drastically. The ending of the book in particular was reduced. What remains is so perfect in its way that the omissions must have been wisely made. As it appears in the final version the ending is in two parts: the meeting under the cover of darkness that Clélia grants to Fabrice. It is a sexual meeting, but carried out with such happiness and modesty (*Entre ici, ami de mon coeur*) that the passage is a poem on the mystery of sexual consummation. It is a dream preceding the real ending where omens are justified and prophecies realized. The tone of the text is so elevated that one accepts the death of Fabrice and the death of Gina as events we had been expecting from the beginning.

The title of the book, *La Chartreuse de Parme*, which until this final point had not been named, serves its real function as a grave, the real grave of the characters and the symbol of the end. But the preparation throughout the book has been so meticulously and inoffensively done that what might have been the sadness of death for the reader becomes the souce of a meditation on life. . . . When he wrote *La Chartreuse de Parme*, Stendhal was such a master of his

style that the kind of writing that might be called improvization for a far less skilled writer was for him a literary
creation that needed very few revisions.

Among the many commentaries Balzac sets forth in his
article on *La Chartreuse,* one in particular seems fully
justified. It is the comparison of Stendhal's novel with Machiavelli's *Il Principe:* "the kind of novel Machiavelli would
have written, had he been exiled from Italy in the nineteenth century." The personal lives in the novel are set
within a very complete picture of the society of the nineteenth century. *La Chartreuse* is both novel and political
treatise. The inventions of Stendhal are carried out in terms
of what he understands about the political-social situation of
the period's history. Balzac was keenly aware of this, because it is a major part of his own theories concerning the
writing of a novel. The character of Mosca, for example, is
somewhat due to Stendhal's understanding of the character
and the role of Metternich. It is not at all an exaggerated
viewpoint to look upon Stendhal as a political novelist in
the tradition of Machiavelli.

Stendhal's long answer to Balzac's article has been published by Martineau in the tenth volume of the correspondence. He explains that he does not write in accordance
with a plan, that he does not consider at any length the way
in which he will write and the organization of his material.
The drawing up of a plan would be an obstacle for him, he
says. His regimen was simple. He would dictate from twenty-
five to thirty pages a day, and then seek some form of relaxation in the evening. By the next morning he had forgotten
everything and had to read the last three or four pages composed the previous day in order to begin the new chapter.
But of course Stendhal knew the general outline of his story.
He knew the life of Alessandro Farnese and had only to in-

vent details of the story. Stendhal insisted that the court intrigue (which Balzac wanted to look upon as the principal construction) was only the background for the real subject, namely the life of Fabrice. On that theme Balzac was silent. It is not surprising that Balzac wanted to make *La Chartreuse de Parme* into a Balzacian novel. And this would be difficult. It is understandably a Stendhal novel!

In his art as novelist Stendhal is closer to Proust than to Balzac, in the sense that the major scenes do not build up to some striking dramatic event or carefully timed solution. The art of a Stendhal scene is not the result but the means. We see the characters acting and reacting, and we follow primarily the motivations for their actions and their words. This act is so intriguing that we seldom think: What will happen next? What is this scene going to lead to? Our attention is focused on what is transpiring at the moment.

A scene of high comedy (brilliantly analyzed by Maurice Bardèche in *Stendhal romancier*) dramatically significant (although we forget the drama and follow the comedy) is the meeting between Gina and Prince Ranuce-Ernest. It is Chapter 14, the opening of the second part of the novel. We know already the opposing traits of character of these two people, the vanity and *petitesse* of the prince of Parma and the impressive strength of character of the Duchess Sanseverina, her beauty, and her haughtiness of spirit when haughtiness is called for. The comedy of the scene lies first in the reversal of roles: The prince who by rights should impose his will and incarnate the forceful dignity of his calling is nervous, inarticulate and attentive on trying to remember how his model, Louis XIV, would have behaved under similar circumstances. The duchess becomes the ruler and the prince becomes the suppliant. Every detail of the scene brings out the comic elements. We follow the struggle

between vanity and forcefulness, and almost forget the reason for the interview, the effort to liberate Fabrice.

There is even more richness of detail and invention in the
scene of Fabrice's escape, with its beautifully sketched noc-
turnal background. Soldiers, in a state of drunkenness, are
singing. A heavy fog rises up from the Po River and covers
the embankment and the *terrasse*. The stark realism of the
scene is offset by poetic effects. The rope, used in the escape,
becomes entangled. Fabrice's emotion is so strong and so
wearing on him that at one point in his descent from his
tower prison, he falls asleep on a platform. His body scrapes
against the wall. Birds fly off from between his legs. Down
below, in the countryside, Gina stands ready to help, with a
group of men. In such a scene, Stendhal is eminently a story-
teller. He imagines countless details and invents them joy-
ously, vigorously. His details (as opposed to those in the art
of Balzac) are used in the build-up of actions, in explaining
the causes of actions.

Because of his experience in writing *Armance, Le Rouge
et le Noir* and *Lucien Leuwen*, Stendhal was in possession
of a technique that permitted him in *La Chartreuse de
Parme* to follow his instincts and give himself over to the
painting of a freer wider canvas. At this point in his career,
he was able to choose from his many exercises in writing
and from his study of other writers his own style of writing
and his own methods of composing a novel. These methods,
fully tested in his past and naturally appropriated by Stendhal, were the constant use of personal memories, the elaborate depiction of a setting in which an action would finally
take place, and the ever-increasing facility in inventing details. These ways of writing, these methods, ended by becoming instinctive and pleasurable. Stendhal had learned
how to establish a physical landscape and a moral climate for

the transpiring of deeds and events. Landscape, climate (both physical and moral) and action are always fused. In *La Chartreuse*, Stendhal no longer has to wonder how to fuse these elements. He creates them already fused, already deriving life and meaning from one another. There were no longer rules to follow, there was simply the novel to compose. He had finally reached his fullest art: the composing of history and the use of the most secret memories and confidences that a man can have.

The absence of any trace of awkward contrivance in the major scenes of *La Chartreuse* and the resilience of such enchanting characters as Gina Sanseverina, Fabrice del Dongo and Count Mosca, must have given to Stendhal the assurance that he had realized some of his most cherished dreams when he had studied and admired certain artistic traits and accomplishments in the art of Molière and Shakespeare. Some of that subtle luminosity he had observed and praised in the painting of Corregio, he had finally been able to capture in his medium of words. He had learned that a detail in a scene of fiction is of little significance unless it is illuminated in such a way that it seems natural and justified. Whatever he uses in *La Chartreuse*—personal memories, historic documents, or sheer inventions of his mind—his power of transcribing and using such elements is the power of a master. He demonstrates the serenity of a master in the control of his craft: in actions, portraits, dialogues, emotions, landscapes, human weaknesses and ambitions, human passions.

How are Stendhal's readers, those he looked upon as the "happy few," able to absorb so much at once and retain so much from the past experiences in the novel as they read the moment-to-moment experiences? How do we fuse the immediate experience we are reading with all that preceded and prepared it? This is, of course, the key question for all fiction. We have to follow Fabrice's escape from the Farnese Tower without forgetting all that has happened to Fabrice heretofore. What means does the novelist employ to permit us a concentration on the event taking place and the total recall of what has already taken place? In other words, what unity presides over Fabrice del Dongo that allows the reader to see him, follow him, and become passionately interested in him?

The source of the book's unity is to be found in Stendhal's very skillful use of symbols or emblems. Marcel Proust was among the first commentators to point out the importance of a sense of height, of altitude, of dizziness that Stendhal emphasizes. In *Le Rouge et le Noir* the themes of walls and ladders and Julien's position on horseback carry with them the effect of danger and precipitation, of mounting ambition and of threatened fall. In *La Chartreuse de Parme*, it is a comparable object or symbol that presides over the book, as Harry Levin says in *The Gates of Horn:* the citadel of Parma, on which the Farnese Tower rests, at the top of which is Fabrice's cell. There, high above the city, Fabrice makes love to Clélia by signs through peepholes. The scene is a memorable admixture of a dominating and dangerous site, of principal characters all related in different ways to this site and of sentiments that are intense and frustrated, all the more intense because they are frustrated.

There, at the top of the tower, Fabrice savors a happiness that he had not known previously. He had dreaded the tower because it had appeared as an ominous portent in the prophetic vision of Abbé Blanès. The thrilling vision at the end of the novel is Fabrice's sense of recalling the highest degree of happiness in the dreaded tower. The type of reader able to participate in such an excitement as this emblem provides belongs to that little band of initiates to whom the book is inscribed at the end by the novelist himself: "to the happy few," a phrase discovered by Stendhal, not in Shakespeare's *Henry V,* but in Oliver Goldsmith's *Vicar of Wakefield,* Chapter 2. For the happy few, improvisation in the book becomes realization. The symbol of the tower gives strong support to the omens of Abbé Blanès. The narrative sketchiness of episodes is strengthened by the power of emblems to survive in the narrative and in the minds of the readers.

The day spent in Grianta by Fabrice is not only a day of prophecy—when Abbé Blanès predicts, by means of his horoscope, the emprisonment to come, a crime that will be perpetrated in the effort to liberate Fabrice and death that will come to him only after he has withdrawn from the world—it is also Fabrice's return to his childhood, to important scenes associated with his past. In the Grianta campanile, Fabrice sees in a vision what will happen to him later in the Farnese Tower. Even the happiness he is to find in the Torre Farnese is foreseen.

Fabrice has returned to Grianta at a moment in his life when he is dissatisfied with everything, when he is worried over his feelings about Gina. He needs to consult his spiritual director Abbé Blanès and at the same time relive the sensations of his earlier life and innocence. The priest advises that Fabrice remain alone in the belfry for an entire day. This experience of loneliness is to be a lesson on the nature of his life and his character, a means by which to face his past and his future, an exercise in meditation and divination.

The following morning, Fabrice is awakened, as has been

predicted, by the church bells ringing at ten o'clock. He is be-
wildered at first and believes he had come to the end of the
world. From the campanile he begins to examine the gardens
below and the courtyard of the château: the potted orange
trees and the sparrows hopping among them in search of
crumbs. When he looks out over the lake and the Alps,
memories of his childhood well up in his mind. The view of
the mountains recalls scenes of his distant past and these
help to clarify scenes of his immediate past. This is addi-
tional help to the spiritual advice of his priestly friend.

The mountains and the tower will be recapitulated in the
torre Farnese episode. There are other parallels between the
Grianta and the Parma towers: the wooden cage of Fabrice's
cell in Parma and Abbé Blanès' observatory called *une cage
de planches*. Fabrice is awakened in Grianta by bells and in
Parma by a dog barking. Potted orange trees are in both
scenes, and the sparrows of Grianta are replaced by the caged
birds Clélia feeds at her window. The height of the belfry
permits Fabrice to see more clearly into the past and into
the future. It is the preparation for his attitude in the tower
where, in order to preserve his happiness, he is willing to
abandon thoughts of escape.

Grianta is the turning point in the story of *La Chartreuse
de Parme*, where Fabrice acquires a sense of meaning in his
life, where he turns away from his haphazard and wandering
life as illustrated in the Waterloo scene, to a more deliberate
quest for happiness—which will be illustrated by his adventures with Marietta and Fausta and by his attachment to
Gina—until he finally meets Clélia.

Before his night spent in the Grianta campanile, Fabrice
pays a visit to the chestnut tree (*marronnier*) that was
planted by his mother the winter of his birth. The early
budding of this tree has once been interpreted by Fabrice

as a sign that he should join Napoleon. He kisses the new
leaves and, before leaving, digs up the soil around the roots.
On his second return he notices that one of the main
branches is broken. He cuts it off with a knife and again digs
up the ground around the tree.

Martin Turnell, in his chapter on Stendhal in *The Novel
in France,* looks upon the tree as phallic and the broken
branch as representing a castration complex. Stephen Gilman, in his article "The Tower as Emblem," interprets the
broken branch as "the unusable portion of Fabrice's past,"
and the digging up of the ground as a preparation for the
future. Henri Martineau, in his edition of the novel, offers
a still different interpretation in calling the broken branch
the announcement of the death of Fabrice's son, Sandrino,
which occurs at the end of *La Chartreuse.*

Alessandro Farnese (the historical model for Fabrice) did
escape from the actual citadel of Parma, according to the
document that Stendhal consulted. To the citadel, Stendhal
added the *tour Farnèse,* a structure both tower and prison.
These are recognizable and facile symbols for man's isolation from other men. In Plato, the body of a man is described as the prison of his soul, as a prison that prevents the
soul from mounting to heaven. But a tower is not always a
prison isolation. It has often been a place for study and work,
as in Montaigne's tower, and Vigny's château, called by
Sainte-Beuve *la tour d'ivoire.*

For Stendhal, the tower, first in Grianta, and then in
Parma, would seem to be a complex symbol, illustrating
both man's need for isolation and that place where he is
able to reach a recognition, a realization of himself. Prison
becomes, paradoxically, a place of liberation. In it, Fabrice
finds the love he had been looking for all his life. There are,
in short, many references, not only in *La Chartreuse de*

Parme but, in letters of Stendhal, to the happiness that may be derived from incarceration in a tower. (*cf.* Harry Levin, *La Citadelle de Parme, Revue de littérature comparée,* 1938, pp. 348–350, and Stephen Gilman, *The Tower as Emblem.*)

One of the new French critics, Jean Starobinski, in an article first published in *Les Temps Modernes,* 1951, entitled *Stendhal pseudonyme,* attaches this pervasive theme of claustration to the imprisonment a proper name signifies and to Stendhal's use of so many pseudonyms. A pseudonym is an evasion too, and, once adopted, turns into a prison. The name of a man, his physical body, and his social class are all prisons. So, the Farnese tower might be looked upon as an architectural pseudonym. There Fabrice finally knows the fullest experience of love, and this is, in the interpretation studied by Starobinski, a fantasy of Stendhal, his dream of being loved, despite his unattractiveness and his age. Whereas Plato and medieval writers described the body as a prison from which the soul longed to escape, Stendhal interpreted a prison as that place that the soul does not want to leave.

In *La Prisonnière,* where Proust analyzes the theme of altitude he finds throughout the work of Stendhal, he equates it with the novelist's spiritual life. The belfry where Abbé Blanès studies astronomy and the *torre Farnese* where Fabrice is a prisoner are places of great height, providing the hero with a self-knowledge that he would not have in another kind of site. This height does not represent for the Stendhalian hero the danger that it does in the myth of Icarus. It is a liberation for the mind and the spirit. It offers an ecstatic experience. It is the place where Fabrice leaves below him, far below in the citadel, the spies and enemies, the threats and warnings about his life. The Farnese tower is Fabrice's peace of mind, as Julien's *rocher* in the forest of Vergy is that place of peacefulness from which he contemplates the power of a hawk in the sky and looks up at it as a possible sign of his destiny. In order to be experienced, happiness has to be imprisoned in a high place, as in a mountain cave for Julien Sorel or in a cell of the Farnese tower for Fabrice del Dongo.

On successive readings of *La Chartreuse de Parme*, the richness and the ambiguities of Fabrice's character become clearer. He is an extraordinary fictional creation, as much an "outsider" as Julien is, despite all his advantages of birth and wealth. He is the outsider not for social reasons but for psychological reasons and because of the ever-varying attitudes of Stendhal toward him. He plays so many roles in the novel, that he grows into an archetypal hero, the hero of heroes, as elusive and as representative as a folklore hero.

His mysterious birth is reminiscent of folklore, and his initiation to life is, characteristically, the test of courage and the taste for adventure in the brilliantly worked out Waterloo episode. His motivation was a yearning to follow his hero Napoleon, but his role on the historic day was that of the innocent, of the ingenuous hero who does not comprehend what is happening, and who, after all is over, wonders whether or not he did reach the battle scene. The episode is a mixture of comic opera, when Fabrice tries unsuccessfully to load his musket, and of touching idealism in his attempts to find his model and hero.

These traits of nobility, innocence, comedy and charm are never lost sight of in the many subsequent adventures that mold Fabrice into one of the really complex human beings in fiction, in whom all the familiar hopes and trials of a young man's life are recorded. He has a fundamental religious faith and a fundamental belief in human goodness, but he commits most of the sins without ever seeing how they contradict his principles. At the beginning of the book, Fabrice's behavior at Waterloo, and at the end of the book, his love for Clélia, demonstrate the noblest traits of his character. They overshadow all the rest. Adultery, fornication and even simony are never presented as seriously as are the outbursts of idealism and love.

He suffers from the tyranny of his father and his brother in a way that is not unlike the suffering of Julien Sorel. Each hero of Stendhal escapes from time to time into nature, into a forest, for example, or to the banks of a lake to forget the malevolence of men. These symbols of his inner life are psychological labyrinths where he wanders in attempts to understand himself. At such moments Fabrice tries to fathom his affection for Gina and touches on the theme of incest. He touches also on a very deepseated fear of sexual impotence. Does he have the physical capacity for real love? The symbolism of the chestnut tree is perhaps best understood in these terms: *il faisait un énorme détour pour aller voir son arbre.* His attentiveness to the broken branch and the ground at the roots of the *marronnier* are easily comprehensible in terms of Fabrice's relationship with his father and brother and of his doubts over his sexual potency. The tree itself, as the symbol of life, is attended to by Fabrice as if he were enacting a ceremony, an actual fertility rite.

If we continue with the motif of tree-pruning, we might say that Fabrice is more drastically cut off from society than the two characters who are foils for his temperament as well as fully developed, fully intriguing personalities themselves: Gina and Mosca. Gina is the thoroughly feminine Fabrice, as courageous as her nephew, but rooted in society and compromised by it. Her incestuous love for Fabrice is never placated. Mosca is the thoroughly virile Fabrice, older and therefore more deeply jealous as a lover and lost in the exciting and debilitating adventures of politics. Clélia too is Fabrice but without his fear of impotence. She, like Fabrice, will stop at nothing in order to preserve in her heart the image of her love.

The happiness that all four characters pursue is as elusive as life itself. But this pursuit of happiness forms the book. It is depicted by Stendhal as desirable and inevitable. The two women and Count Mosca are so involved with social and political commitments that their pursuit is intermittent. Fabrice is the true protagonist whose pursuit is constant. He is the outsider, the hero separated from the world, isolated from it by the intensity and the mysteriousness of his feelings.

IX

Stendhal

AT THE AGE OF TWENTY, in 1803, when Stendhal settled in Paris for his first sojourn of any length of time, he gave every evidence of a lack of sympathy with the new style of writing called *le romantisme*. Chateaubriand's *Le Génie du Christianisme*, published in 1802, was a massive work, one of the most noteworthy publishing successes of the century, which, in its themes, its rhetoric and the sensibility it analyzed, was, more than any other single work, to train and inspire the talents of Lamartine, Hugo, Musset and a countless number of minor writers. But Stendhal, born just a few years earlier than the major figures of the first generation of French romantic writers, remained independent of Chateaubriand's formidable influence. The literary style of *Le Rouge et le Noir* was the antithesis of that of *René* by Chateaubriand and Mme. de Staël's *Delphine*.

At the age of forty, in 1823, when Stendhal returned to Paris from Milan, for a second period of some duration, this time for approximately ten years, he was still impervious to the new work of the romantics, to the first volume of romantic poetry, for example, *Les Méditations Poétiques* of Lamartine, of 1820, the second major success in nineteenth-century publishing. His first books were behind him, exercises on music, painting and tourist reports on Italy: *Vies de Haydn, Mozart et de Métastase* (1815), *Histoire de la peinture en Italie* (1817), and *Rome, Naples et Florence* (1817). His style in these first books was closer to Napoleon's (in the letters and the *bulletins*) than to Chateaubriand's. In fact, in 1817 Stendhal had begun a biography of the exiled emperor (*Vie de Napoléon*) and later he acknowledged his indebtedness to the neutral quality and the impersonality of Napoleon's *code civil*. After all, Stendhal belonged to the military generation at the turn of the century rather than to the first generation of romantic writers. He had studied at one of the first *écoles centrales,* founded in accord with the philosophical and scientific ideal of the Revolution.

When the balance is drawn up, Stendhal appears as a failure with his contemporaries. Wasn't he, in spirit at least, a Milanese rather than a Frenchman? Like Napoleon he had in his background a Franco-Italian ancestry. Throughout the early years of his career, he never relinquished his hope of becoming a second Molière, even as Balzac had hoped at the same time in his life to become a second Corneille. To his writing on music, painting and tourism, he had added a literary manifesto, *Racine et Shakespeare* (1825), and more personal writings that today, in the light of his subsequent work, reveal his central vocation—one comparable to Montaigne's in the history of French literature—that of self-knowledge, of self-discovery. All of Stendhal's writings are analyses of his ego. *De l'amour* (1822) was one of those analyses. But if Stendhal had not written his five novels, all his other works, including the *Vie de Rossini* (1823), the *Prome-*

nades dans Rome (1829), the *Chroniques italiennes* and the frankly personal writings—the *Journal* and *Vie de Henry Brulard*—would doubtless have sunk into oblivion.

Prior to *Armance*, Stendhal had grown into a somewhat obese, florid *bon vivant*, obsessed with strategies for feminine conquests. He was the prototype of the bachelor writer, the would-be adventurer in love and in life, the epicurean who is easily duped, the lover of literature, music, painting and good cooking. The seven years in Milan, 1814 to 1821, had initiated him to the pleasures of the senses and the pleasures of the mind, to a freedom of the spirit, to a love of landscapes and natural beauty as well as to a love of the arts. Like Balzac, Stendhal drew up plan after plan for the conduct of his life. The bachelor is the perpetual adolescent whose obsessive calculations often drain him of sufficient energy to carry out planned escapades or planned work. Stendhal wanted, more than anything else, to be a creative writer, but he often suffocated under his pile of notes and cards, under the endless preparation he believed necessary to become a writer. His self-imposed discipline was a form of sterility.

Nothing in the early books indicated traits that would make of Stendhal a world writer. The first book on the lives of three composers (Haydn, Mozart and Metastasio) was not ever a work plagiarized from the writings of Carpani. It was an unacknowledged translation. The history of Italian painting was the work of an amateur, made up of notes, reflections and transcriptions from other critics. A Stendhalian theme emerges from the book on the three Italian cities: the happiness that comes to the spectator as he contemplates the landscapes of Italy. There are no passages of panegyric in Stendhal's attempts to write a life of Napoleon, first in 1818 and then later, in 1838. But Napoleon becomes a mythic figure for three of Stendhal's fictional characters: for Julien

(*Le Rouge et le Noir*), for Lucien (*Lucien Leuwen*) and for Fabrice (*La Chartreuse de Parme*).

He was a writer who first did not write literature. He wrote on painting. He wrote, for England, journalistic articles on newly published books. He wrote on social manners and customs. He recorded anecdotes on human types encountered in various salons. He was to come upon his real career in a very circuitous, very oblique way, by *la voie oblique,* a phrase explored by two of the most astute critics of Stendhal, Harry Levin and Victor Brombert.

The perpetual wanderings of Stendhal—from country to country, from one hotel to another—and his perpetual use of pseudonyms (according to the latest count, Henri Beyle of Grenoble, France, used close to two hundred names) testify to a quest or a pilgrimage of a psychological if not a mystical nature. It is the quest of every major writer, who by nature is a compulsive writer, who has to write and who never knows when he is writing whether this is *his* work, whether this will be *his* work. This restless itinerant Stendhal believed he found himself first in Italy, as Byron believed he found himself in Greece, as Gide believed he found himself in North Africa. What Stendhal described as the *dolce far niente* atmosphere of Milan caused him to forget, intermittently, at least, the bourgeois family background of Grenoble and the severely compartmentalized social life of Paris. In order to offset the provincial sentimentalist in him, Henri Beyle needed to live in other climates and to bear other names than his own. In order to become a writer, he had to learn to play the part of the sophisticated cynic. Little wonder that he was drawn so forcibly in his younger years to *Don Quixote*. Henri Beyle of Grenoble and Milan experienced all the incongruities of temperament and of life that are associated with the Spanish hero of Cervantes.

Stendhal is the supreme example of the writer who became his books. Not consciously, of course, but subconsciously the happiness he sought from life and that perpetually eluded him was found by him at last in the writing and the dictating of his books and, in particular, of his two master-pieces: *Le Rouge et le Noir* and *La Chartreuse de Parme*. These books are novels, but they are also treatises on ways of the world, mythical projections of the way in which Henri Beyle had learned to live in the world, both realistically and imaginatively. Writing grew into Stendhal's happiness, into that form of happiness he was unable to achieve in any literal sense.

The background of these two novels of the writer's happiness is as complex as that of any other masterpiece. The literary background is in *Don Quixote* and Molière, in *Orlando Furioso* and *La Nouvelle Héloïse* and *Les Liaisons Dangereuses*. The philosophical background is in that science of ideas called ideology, which looks back to the eighteenth-century encyclopedists and ahead to the nineteenth-century positivists. This study taught him that man is the product of all the circumstances of his life. Untiringly Stendhal rehearsed in his personal writings, and to some extent in all of his writings, these circumstances: his family life, the intellectual discipline of reading and experiments in the writing of comedies, his deliberate attempts to live as a cosmopolitan rather than as a French nationalist, his poses of dandy in Parisian and Italian salons, his lack of feeling for poetry, his dislike for the rhetorical prose of Chateaubriand.

Everything in the fifty-nine years that Stendhal lived is the story of a writer, because nothing in that life was useless for the writer. The child, the adolescent and the man were the writer whose taste did not change but progressed and deepened. Everything he attempted as critic, journalist, historian, novelist simply meant that he was the writer and nothing but the writer. His study of man's variability and complexity was pursued throughout his life for the sole purpose of being a writer.

The fondness Stendhal showed for memoirs and anecdotes, as well as for the *novelle* he came upon in reading Italian Renaissance manuscripts, testified to a writer's attitude and attentiveness and inclinations. This fondness clearly indicated one of his major traits of a writer: his dependence on documentation rather than on inventiveness and imagination. The substance of his books he took from every possible source, from chance readings, from stories heard in a conversation, from newspaper articles. Like Molière before him and like André Gide three-quarters of a century after him, he made into his own the writings of others and the scandal reports of his day. The use of cutout newspaper items—of *coupures*, as the French call them—is significant for both *Le Rouge et le Noir* of Stendhal and *Les Faux-Monnayeurs* of Gide.

A critical attitude toward the living and the dead characterized Stendhal's mind, as it did Gide's also. The prototype of this mind was Montaigne's whose mobility of thought and alertness made him into a man impatient to live and understand, to feel and enjoy whatever came to his attention. Stendhal's mind, like Gide's and Montaigne's, was in a constant state of examination: attentive to what was happening outside of him and attentive at the same time to the manner in which these happenings were affecting him. The word *egotism* and even the more pejorative term *egoism* have been applied to all three writers, egotism especially to Stendhal because he used it himself in the title of one of his autobiographical works, *Souvenirs d'égotisme*. But the word thus used by Stendhal in his title is ironic. He is interested in his reaction to everything, but in a detached and almost scientific way. He demonstrates no self-complacency, no self-indulgence in his "egotistical" exercises. He is the observer and the self-observer, and, like his ancestor Montaigne and his successor Gide, such observation is a form of discipline, a form almost of stubbornness carried out in order to reach lucidity.

Today, thanks to the labors of many scholars, we probably know more about Stendhal than he knew about himself. We certainly see the general pattern of his life more clearly than he did and the genesis of the writer in his life. Looked at objectively, his life was a series of failures: a childhood, which after his mother's death, was sombre and stifled; an experience in warfare that never developed and never provided a feeling of exaltation; literary enterprises that inevitably turned out to be disappointing; futile infatuations over women and love affairs that were fiascos; syphilis, contracted early and never cured; the diplomatic appointment to Città Vecchia, at the end of his life, and which was in reality a semidisgrace; a loss of hair and increasing obesity which made him more unattractive physically, the loneliness of the bachelor living in hotel rooms or small furnished apartments.

Yes, a depressing balance sheet of failures for any man, but failures that, in the case of Stendhal, were offset by a mysterious and indomitable sense of happiness. For him, happiness consisted in a capacity to reason lucidly about the world he observed around him. He would say that it lies in a man's will to reason with logic and justice about all matters, and in his mind to feel deeply about these matters and to react to them with peacefulness and vibrancy. This kind of happiness implies a background of sadness. What the world designates as failure is indispensable for this type of reasoning and reasonable happiness that is visible just beyond the site of failure. No! Stendhal was not a self-worshipper. Such a phrase as *le culte du moi,* or the cult of the ego, the cult of the egotist, is inappropriate in his case. He cultivated the ego, trained it and deepened it. But this is vastly different. It is the difference between *un culte* and *une culture.*

Of the five novels of Stendhal, two seem to us today clearly masterpieces, and one, *Armance,* very close to a masterpiece. If Stendhal was hopelessly a failure in his attempts to write for the stage, his place is very high in the history of the French novel, not only in the achievements of the novels that have won, and continue to win, admirers for over one hundred years, but also in the creation or the renovation of a literary form. One hesitates to use any one term to describe this form: a conversation-novel? an improvised novel? It is a novel that seems to rehearse itself and create itself as it expands and contracts, as it vocalizes as if in preparation for a performance. The best scenes are close to comedy scenes and one realizes that the efforts Stendhal spent in writing plays come to fruition in the dramatic scenes of his novels. The characters act out their parts. The reader sees them in action and he himself reaches his conclusions about the motivations of their actions and does not need to be told what the motivations are.

In order to clarify and explain a character, Stendhal carries on a perpetual transposition in his art of a novelist. He transposes the idea of a character into an act that the character usually performs in a group. We watch therefore acts that are not articulated or analyzed by words but that are performed as on a stage. The reader (or the spectator) has to collaborate with the novelist in deducing meanings and interpretations. A small and seemingly insignificant fact in a man's life can thus open out into a vast perspective of meanings. It is literally able to create a universe by itself, a fictional universe.

In this technique of improvisation, which has been brilliantly studied by Jean Prévost, Stendhal the writer does not appear as the omniscient narrator. The protagonist takes first place. Out of the consciousness of the protagonist the novel is improvised and created. Stendhal the narrator does not know what is coming next in the narrative. He has to wait for the consciousness of the protagonist to open up the way. Stendhal is thus the forerunner of two closely related developments of the French novel in the twentieth century: the first, which might be called the "impertinent" novel of Gide (*Les Caves du Vatican,* 1914), of Jean Cocteau (*Thomas l'imposteur,* 1923) and of Raymond Radiguet (*Le bal du comte d'Orgel,* 1924). The heroic propensities and impertinences of Stendhal's Fabrice are recast in Gide's Lafcadio. The two heroes exercise a similar freedom of thought and movement and cast the same kind of spell or enchantment over those people they encounter. They move ahead from one activity to another, from one episode to another without regard for the past, without following any preordained schedule of their creator. Cocteau's Thomas and his two *enfants terribles,* Paul and Elisabeth, scorn the routine ways of their society and create a world of their own in their *chambre.* Radiguet, even more than Gide and Cocteau, created characters and an atmosphere in his second novel, *Le bal du comte d'Orgel,* that are fashioned on *Armance.*

Forerunner of the impertinent novel of World War I and postwar literature (1915–1926), Stendhal has also served as one of the guides to the *nouveau roman* of the 1950s in

France, in the writing of Alain Robbe-Grillet, Nathalie
Sarraute and Claude Simon, where psychology is not discussed as such, but where it is visible solely in the action of
the characters, in their gestures, in their glances, in the words
they speak. Stendhal is the first and perhaps the greatest to
date of the nondiscursive psychologists among French
novelists. The restraint he demonstrates in describing human motivations has been closely watched and followed by
novelists coming two or three generations after his death,
as he himself predicted: by Gide, Cocteau and Radiguet,
first, and then by the so-called "new novelists" who learned
from him how to allow a scene in a salon or a *café*, in a
room or on a street to reveal or partially reveal the inner
life of a human being.

The new element in Stendhal criticism of the past twenty
years is an ever-increasing interest in and admiration for
Armance. The introduction Gide wrote for an edition of
Armance has without much doubt counted greatly in this
new focusing on Stendhal's first novel. A second explanation, which has counted less widely than Gide's introduction
but even more pointedly for some readers of Stendhal, was
Radiguet's brief novel, *Le bal du comte d'Orgel,* where the
two characters of the count and François present striking
resemblances to Octave.

Radiguet claimed that his novel was patterned on *La
Princesse de Clèves,* on the story of a woman totally noble in
her actions who remains faithful to her husband whom she
loves, even when she feels for another man a stronger and
more passionate love. This is the situation in Mme. de Lafayette's novel, in the triangle of the princess, the prince and
the duc de Nemours. In *Le bal du comte d'Orgel,* the count
is married to Mahaut who is loved by François. The situa-

tion is identical. There is only one male protagonist in the Stendhal work, Octave, who guards his fatal secret with an aristocratic aloofness that is also visible in Radiguet's count and who feels the same kind of passionate love for Armance that François feels for Mahaut. The secret of the seeming coldness of the count remains to the end as mysterious as Octave's secret. The blunt explanation given by Stendhal in his letter to Mérimée is only a facile explanation of a deeper and more enigmatic secret. Impotence may take many forms, and it is more reasonable for us today to see in Octave's implied sexual impotence something more moral than physical.

Octave, after all, is remarkably presented by Stendhal as the victim of a dying society. He is a *fin-de-race* type of young man who may well incarnate the futility of the Restoration more than he exemplifies a fear of failure in sexual intercourse. The terms are not in the least equivocal by which Stendhal states in his letter to Mérimée how Octave, once married with Armance, might have circumvented impotency and given his wife sexual pleasure. Octave's secret quite literally died with him on the boat in sight of the land of Greece.

The appeal of *Armance* today lies in the power of its enigma. What is not said by Octave is far more important than what is said by him. Nothing is left unexplained in such psychological novels as *Manon Lescaut* and *Adolphe*. In such romantic novels as *La Nouvelle Héloïse* and *René*, we know exactly why the hero feels as he does. But with *Armance*, the way is opened up for the modern hero who is, in the last analysis, inexplicable to himself and to others. The list is impressively long of aristocratic, aloof, impertinent, nondescript heroes who reveal very little concerning the essential part of themselves: Gide's *Lafcadio* (*Les caves du Vatican*), Proust's Robert de Saint-Loup (*A la recherche du temps perdu*), Mauriac's Raymond (*Le Désert de l'Amour*), Graham Greene's Pinkie (*Brighton Rock*), Camus' Meursault (*L'Etranger*), Michel Butor's Léon (*La Modification*), Beckett's Molloy, the major in Carson McCuller's *Reflections in a Golden Eye.* . . . In the case of each of these heroes, beginning with Stendhal's Octave, the world is seen by a human being who fundamentally believes he is separated from the world, and from the world's happiness.

The story of Julien Sorel will always appeal to a wider public than the equivocal story of Octave. *Le Rouge et le Noir* is the central book of Stendhal, far richer in its treatment of human life than would ever have been imagined on its publication in 1830. The very title, with its strong antithesis of colors, seems to be announcing the two extremes of human life, of which one will be lost and one gained, as in a game of chance: happiness or unhappiness.

During the fifty-two days when Stendhal dictated *La Chartreuse de Parme,* he was transformed by becoming Fabrice, or at least by creating Fabrice. At that moment in his life, Stendhal was a civil servant, a functionary who had been assigned an insignificant post of consul. Unsuccessful in love, far from enjoying any eminent success in society, he wrote, as a triumph over all of his shortcomings and disappointments, his picaresque novel of passion and pursuit.

Stendhal encourages his readers to guess more than he tells them directly. His writing does not have the fullness and clarity of Flaubert, nor does it have the realistic details and exposition of Balzac. Parma, for example, in *La Chartreuse* is never described, but the atmosphere of the small city is suggested. The same principle is followed by Stendhal in his study of human character. There is an obvious search for pleasure and happiness in all of his characters. *Beylisme* and *égotisme*, without forming a doctrine, do signify a form of epicureanism that stimulates a Stendhal character each day to begin over again the game of existence. But in the background of this search there is an accumulation of bitterness, of disappointments, of failures that adds to the search for happiness, that tends to darken the search and the possibility for reaching happiness. This seeming contradiction accounts for the lack of clarity in the human characterizations of Stendhal's novels. They are ambiguous, and at no time in their existences can they be seen as motivated by one drive, by one ambition. If happiness is the goal, then that which constitutes happiness is impossible to define once and for all. It changes with the color of the sky and with the minute and drastic changes in the politics of man.

Despite the famous sentence in *Racine et Shakespeare* where Stendhal claims that a political idea in a literary work is comparable to a pistol shot in a concert (*Toute idée politique dans un ouvrage de littérature . . . est un coup de pistolet au milieu d'un concert*), Stendhal's political viewpoint, in its highest sense and not merely the politics of a given moment in history, has tremendous importance in his novels. And behind the more restricted political philosophy of Stendhal, lies a moral-sociological philosophy of man that colors all of his treatment of human nature and history. The characters he created and their search for happiness are inexplicable without Stendhal's fundamental belief in progress. Progress in all domains: politics, morality, aesthetics. Stendhal believed in the doctrine of human perfectibility. This doctrine is in itself an enigma, because of all the wars and setbacks and defeats the human spirit has undergone and continues to undergo. Everything that Stendhal wrote points to this conviction that the history of man is the history of his progress and that man will continue to progress. The human mind is perfectible. Again, in this important aspect of Stendhal's thought, Montaigne is the precursor and Gide, the successor. Even in the domain of religious thought, the resemblances among these three writers are significant. Stendhal was steadfastly anticlerical, but not antireligious. He despised in Catholicism a religion that could be utilized and exploited by the ruling class. But Christianity, in the figure and the example of Christ, was a factor that counted for Stendhal in the history of human progress. Such a view is harmonious with that of Montaigne and Gide. The parish priest Chélan, in *Le Rouge et le Noir,* and Abbé Blanès, in *La Chartreuse,* are figures of paternal goodness and charity.

Politics is the immediate means by which progress can be maintained or interrupted. Even Napoleon was looked upon by Stendhal as a factor in the progress of mankind. Even when he took on the traits of a despot, he was the enlightened despot who had interpreted the Revolution as the cause of the regeneration of the European way of life. Stendhal's political beliefs—his Jacobinism—are closely related to his hopes for moral and aesthetic development. Julien Sorel, the young hero from the proletariat and Ferrante Palla, the *carbonaro,* represent a resurgence against despotism. In the history of sociological writing, Stendhal's *Mémoires d'un touriste* is one of the very first tracts on the lamentable condition of the proletariat. The goal of Stendhal as a commentator on his day and as a writer is to increase in his own way and no matter how slight the degree, the happiness that exists already in the world.

This political view on the progress of man, in its relationship with the moral behavior of man in his slow progress, along with the belief that the ideal of beauty changes and develops with the change and development of each generation, makes of the writings of Stendhal a world in themselves, a recognizable world. There is a Stendhal world, in the sense that there is a Proustian world and a Balzacian world, that is built upon his vision of France and Europe, upon his understanding of certain literary works that preceded him, upon the defeats and disappointments of his personal life and finally upon the style of writing that he developed.

Stubbornly, persistently, throughout his life Stendhal wrote day by day, as if the act of writing represented a *raison d'être* for his existence. What Stendhal sought to recapture in his writing was the honesty of an emotion that otherwise might disappear forever. To recapture an emotion meant reliving not only its dramatic force, but its humor also. There is humor, of an almost Proustian quality, in the scene of the young bishop of Agde watching himself in the mirror and being watched at the same time by Julien. There is humor also in the scene at Waterloo where Fabrice moves in and out of danger and comical situations. But the humor of such scenes is not without its accompanying melancholy. The plight of man is always just behind his ingenuousness. This marriage in Stendhal of pathos with the abruptness of his great *ingénus* is never the celebration of a *mal du siècle,* of any romantic vagueness of spirit or boredom.

The way in which Stendhal presented his characteristic world was almost shocking at the time of the major publications: 1827, 1830, 1839. His style did not show the traditional flow and continuity and ampleness of the then fashionable style of the romantics. It was more staccato in its effect, more interrupted, swifter and more broken. The

French call it *le style du discontinu,* which has been developed in the twentieth century, in the poetry of Apollinaire and in the narrative style of the *nouveau roman.*

Stendhal places side by side exterior events and musings about the events. His descriptions of objects and places are usually very brief. His own comments intervene as if they were part of the exterior narrative. His habit of narrating facts and events without always describing the effects of these happenings is a habit of the new novelist of the twentieth century.

The word "improvisation" is far from accurate when used to describe Stendhal's style. He wrote (or dictated) in the passion of the moment, and his long practice of writing served him well under those conditions. Rhythmic variations of the sentences, rather than metaphor or choice of words, account for the vitality of Stendhal's lean writing. Writing was his happiness. And an extraordinary sympathy for his characters is a significant trait in his art of storytelling. Stendhal is the prototype of the novelist: a solitary figure when he writes and solitary in the events of his life. He was quite literally inhabited by the characters he lived with imaginatively and projected into his stories. He saw them around him, felt their suffering, understood their hopes and was able to recreate all that. Stendhal discovered himself as he discovered and created characters within himself. His happiness was a participation in the happiness or unhappiness of others. His use of literature and his practice of literature are succinctly formulated in a remarkable sentence of *Vie de Henry Brulard* (Chapter 15), where he uses the verb *sympathiser,* so vital in an understanding of Stendhal's sensibility: *Je sympathise, comme à dix ans, lorsque je lisais l'Arioste, avec tout ce qui est contes d'amour, de forêts (les bois et leur vaste silence), de générosité.*

It is a startling and revealing choice of terms used by Stendhal in this sentence dominated by the verb "to sympathize with" or "to feel for." At ten, when he first read Ariosto, he was held by the love story, by the descriptions of forests, and by examples of the human impulse of generosity. Into these three words, *contes d'amour, forêts* and *générosité,* Stendhal condenses the first effects of literature on his childhood. But these are also the themes of the mature novelist, if to them we add the political background: the search and the experience of love, the landscapes and the depths of the forests in *Armance,* in *Le Rouge et le Noir,* and in *La Chartreuse de Parme* and, finally, those impulses of nobility and generosity that dominate all the lower impulses in Octave, Julien and Fabrice.

The child Henri Beyle of Grenoble remained in the man Stendhal of Paris, Milan, Rome and Città Vecchia. The three simple terms, discovered by the child reading Ariosto —love, nature and goodness of heart—became more complex in time with the political understanding of the diplomat and with the career man in society. But the novelist, in his accumulation of experiences and disappointments, never lost sight of them. The rich varied complexities and obsessions of Stendhal's life make such terms difficult for us to understand today.

Love would seem to be, if we follow the testimonials of his novels, the deepening of a man's ego and an ever-growing awareness of the idea of the person who is the cause of this deepening. The happiness of love would seem to be the inner experience of being, of having been in the presence of some form of human perfection.

The beauty of landscapes is an experience felt especially by the solitary heroes of Stendhal, who knew themselves to be, in a sense, "outsiders." The light of dawn over the Alps and the sunsets seen by the boy Henri from the terrace of his grandfather's house were experiences that were relived in the composing of the novels: in Julien's forest between Vergy and Verrières, in Lake Como, in the Lombardy landscapes, in the view from the tower of Abbé Blanès. These were spiritual experiences of emancipation for the child and the writer.

Générosité is the hardest, because it is the most volatile, of the three terms to analyze. But it is perhaps the clue to the other terms and to the political significance of Stendhal's novels. It may well be the Stendhalian word for sincerity, for *le naturel,* that frankness and direction in the character of his hero that are constantly breaking through the masks and the poses and the hypocrisies that society forces on a man.

Générosité is perhaps best defined in Stendhal's and his hero's impulse toward truth. Julien Sorel, about to be executed, asks himself questions that have guided his life up to that moment. He loved truth, but has not found it . . . *J'ai aimé la vérité . . . Où est-elle?* (Part II, Chapter 44, pp. 690–93, Pléiade edition). Rather than truth, he found hypocrisy or at least a form of charlatanism even among the most virtuous people. And he concludes, in this first development of his meditation: man cannot trust man . . . *l'homme ne peut pas se fier à l'homme.*

Is truth to be found in religion? he asks. It is perhaps in the heart of a real priest, a man such as Massillon or Fénelon, but the God of such a priest could not be the despot of the Bible, he would be Voltaire's God, just, good, infinite . . . Julien then concludes that this dialogue with himself about God is itself hypocritical, because he is alone and only a few steps away from death. His century has imposed this mask of hypocrisy on him: *O dix-neuvième siècle!*

This entire Chapter 44 of the second part of *Le Rouge et le Noir,* which precedes the final chapter of the work, eloquently demonstrates the diverseness of man's nature according to Stendhal. There is never a last word that can be said on any topic of human experience. In order to live in accordance with this generosity of feeling that seems to be the goal in man's search for happiness, he has to break through and continue breaking through the imprisonment of his name and of his native city. He has to learn to live day by day, not in the imprisonment of his past, but in the freedom of the present. Ironically and dramatically, the strength and the vision that Julien sought during the last five years of his life came to him in prison, at the end of his meditation on God. It is in the final sentence of Chapter 44 that Stendhal shows us Julien at the climactic moment of peace and lucidity: *Julien se sentait fort et résolu comme l'homme qui voit clair dans son âme.*

YADDO, SUMMER 1967
NAPLES AND GRENOBLE, SUMMER 1968

Dates in the Life of Stendhal

1783   Birth of Henri Beyle, in Grenoble, son of Ché-rubin-Joseph Beyle and Caroline-Adélaïde Henriette Gagnon.

1799   At sixteen, won first prize in mathematics at the Ecole Centrale de Grenoble. Went to Paris at the end of the year, on the 19 Brumaire, *an* VIII. Received an army commission.

1800   Left for Italy. Lived in Milan as second lieutenant.

1801   Returned to Paris at the end of the year and resigned from the army.

1802   Grenoble and Paris. Study of languages and acting. Read the *idéologues*.

1805   In Marseille, as lover of Mélanie Louason, actress.

1806   Administrative post in the army. Berlin and Brunswick (Germany).

1808   Brunswick and Paris.

1811   Paris. Life of a dandy.

1812   Paris to Moscow. Participated in the retreat from Moscow.

1814	Fall of Napoleon. Leaves for Milan.
1814–1821	Milan.
1815	*Vies de Haydn, de Mozart et de Métastase.*
1817	*Histoire de la peinture en Italie.*
	Rome, Naples et Florence.
1821–1830	Paris. Literature and society.
1822	*De l'amour.*
1823	*Racine et Shakespeare, première partie.*
	Vie de Rossini.
1825	*Racine et Shakespeare, seconde partie.*
1827	*Armance.*
1829	*Promenades dans Rome.*
1830	*Le Rouge et le Noir.*
	In September, appointed French consul to Trieste.
1831	Trieste. Appointed consul in Città Vecchia.
1831–1836	Città Vecchia and Rome.
1834	Began *Lucien Leuwen.*
1835	Began *Vie de Henry Brulard.*
1836–1839	Leave of absence, spent in Paris.
1838	*Mémoires d'un touriste.*
1839	*La Chartreuse de Parme.*
1839–1841	Città Vecchia. Began *Lamiel.*
1841	Paris.
1842	Death in Paris.

Major Works of Stendhal
Available in French Editions

Oeuvres Complètes, published by Henri Martineau. Le Divan:

Histoire de la peinture en Italie. 2 vol.

Correspondance. 10 vol.

Vies de Haydn, de Mozart et de Métastase. 1 vol.

Vie de Rossini. 2 vol.

Lucien Leuwen. 3 vol.

Le Rouge et le Noir. 2 vol.

La Chartreuse de Parme. 2 vol.

Vie de Henry Brulard. 2 vol.

Souvenirs d'égotisme. 1 vol.

Lamiel. 1 vol.

Rome, Naples et Florence. 1 vol.

De l'amour. 1 vol.

Oeuvres, collection La Pléiade, Gallimard:

I. *Romans. (Armance, Le Rouge et le Noir, Lucien Leuwen)*

II. *Romans. (La Chartreuse de Parme, Chroniques italiennes, Romans et nouvelles)*

III. *Oeuvres intimes. (Vie de Henry Brulard,* etc.)
Correspondance I. 1800–1821
Correspondance II. 1821–1834

Classiques Garnier:
Le Rouge et le Noir
La Chartreuse de Parme
Armance
Vie de Henry Brulard
De l'amour

Major Works of Stendhal
Available in English

Armance. trans. by Gilbert and Suzanne Sale. London, Merlin Press, 1960.

The Chartreuse of Parma. trans. by Lady Mary Loyd. Appleton, 1901.

Lamiel. trans. by T. W. Earp. New Directions, 1952.

The Life of Henry Brulard. trans. by Jean Stewart and B. Knight. London, Merlin Press, 1958.

Life of Rossini. trans. by Richard Coe. Criterion Books, 1957.

Lucien Leuwen. trans. by Louise Varèse. New Directions, 1950.

Memoirs of Egotism. trans. by Hannah and Matthew Josephson. Lear, 1949.

The Private Diaries of Stendhal. trans. by Robert Sage. Doubleday, 1954.

The Red and the Black. trans. by C. K. Scott-Moncrieff. Modern Library, 1953.

Rome, Naples, and Florence. trans. by Richard Coe. Braziller, 1960.

To the Happy Few, Selected Letters of Stendhal. trans. by Norman Cameron. London, Lehmann, 1952.

Critical Studies on Stendhal (*in French*)

Arbalet, Paul, *La Jeunesse de Stendhal,* 2 vol. Champion, 1919.

Balzac, Honoré de, *Oeuvres Complètes,* tome 23. Calmann-Lévy, 1899.

Bardèche, Maurice, *Stendhal romancier.* La Table Ronde, 1947.

Billy, André, *Ce cher Stendhal.* Flammarion, 1958.

Blin, Georges, *Stendhal et les problèmes du roman.* Corti, 1954.

Blum, Léon, *Stendhal et le beylisme,* 3e édition. Albin Michel, 1947.

Bourget, Paul, *Essais de psychologie contemporaine,* tome I. 1883.

Brombert, Victor, *Stendhal et la voie oblique.* Presses Universitaires de France, 1954.

del Litto, Vittorio, *La vie intellectuelle de Stendhal.* Presses universitaires de France, 1959.

Gide, André, *Incidences* (préface à *Armance*). Gallimard, 1924.

Girard, René, *Valéry et Stendhal.* PMLA, June 1954.

Martineau, Henri, *L'oeuvre de Stendhal. Histoire de ses livres et de sa pensée.* Le Divan, 1945.

Critical Studies on Stendhal (*in English*)

Adams, Robert, *Stendhal: Notes on a Novelist*. Noonday Press, 1959; reissued 1968 by Funk & Wagnalls.

Brombert, Victor, ed. *Stendhal, a Collection of Critical Studies*. Prentice-Hall, 1962.

Brombert, Victor, *Stendhal: Fiction and Themes of Freedom*. Random House, 1968.

Denommé, Robert T., "Julien Sorel and the Modern Conscience." *Western Humanities Review*, Summer, 1967.

Gilman, Stephen, "The Tower as Emblem." *Analecta Romanica 22*. Frankfurt, Klostermann, 1967.

Giraud, Raymond, *The Unheroic Hero*. Rutgers Press, 1957.

Grant, Richard B., "The Death of Julien Sorel." *L'Esprit Créateur*, Spring, 1962.

Howe, Irving, *Politics and the Novel*. Horizon Press, 1957.

Josephson, Matthew, *Stendhal or the Pursuit of Happiness*. Doubleday, 1946.

Levin, Harry, *The Gates of Horn*. Oxford, 1963.

Turnell, Martin, *The Novel in France*. New Directions, 1951.

INDEX

Index